T0114671

31-DAY HAPPINESS CHALLENGE

LAW OF ATTRACTION CAMP

CLAUDIA PARRA ROWE

BALBOA.PRESS

A DIVISION OF HAY HOUSE

Copyright © 2022 Claudia Parra Rowe.

All rights reserved. No part of this book may be used or reproduced by any means,
graphic, electronic, or mechanical, including photocopying, recording, taping or by
any information storage retrieval system without the written permission of the author
except in the case of brief quotations embodied in critical articles and reviews.

Balboa Press books may be ordered through booksellers or by contacting:

Balboa Press
A Division of Hay House
1663 Liberty Drive
Bloomington, IN 47403
www.balboapress.com
844-682-1282

Because of the dynamic nature of the Internet, any web addresses or links contained in
this book may have changed since publication and may no longer be valid. The views
expressed in this work are solely those of the author and do not necessarily reflect the views
of the publisher, and the publisher hereby disclaims any responsibility for them.

The author of this book does not dispense medical advice or prescribe the use of any technique as a form of
treatment for physical, emotional, or medical problems without the advice of a physician, either directly or
indirectly. The intent of the author is only to offer information of a general nature to help you in your quest
for emotional and spiritual well-being. In the event you use any of the information in this book for yourself,
which is your constitutional right, the author and the publisher assume no responsibility for your actions.

Any people depicted in stock imagery provided by Getty Images are models,
and such images are being used for illustrative purposes only.
Certain stock imagery © Getty Images.

ISBN: 979-8-7652-3483-9 (sc)
ISBN: 979-8-7652-3484-6 (e)

Print information available on the last page.

Balboa Press rev. date: 10/21/2022

My children have been my primary motivation for this project. And thanks to my husband Steve for his support, advice, and encouragement.

CONTENTS

Hi, I'm Claudia

I have some critical questions for you.

- **Do you ever feel overwhelmed and anxious?**
- Are you often sad, tired, or depressed?
- **Do you lack confidence and have low self-esteem?**
- Do you feel unworthy and undeserving, embarrassed for wanting more?
- **Do you dream of a wonderful relationship or wish to improve your current one?**
- Do you feel stuck in a toxic and abusive relationship?
- **Would you like to get along with family, friends, and workmates?**
- Do you stop yourself from following your dreams with negative self-talk?
- **Do you hate your job but lack the courage to pursue your dreams?**
- Do you feel like you'll never amount to anything?
- **Is money always short, or you can't seem to get out of debt?**
- Are you often ill, engage in unhealthy behavior, and don't like what you see in the mirror?
- **Are you easily angered or annoyed?**
- Do you feel it's too late for you to be, do, or have everything you want?

If you said yes to one more of the above questions, you are not alone. I checked each question at different points in my life.

First, a little about myself:

I created the "31-Day Happiness Challenge" to help others become aware of the powerful "law of attraction." I believe our world can be a better place when, as individuals, we understand the power within to direct our thoughts and actions, discover our true selves, and ascend to a higher level of consciousness, creating positivity, happiness, and peace.

I understand the difficulties that we face. I know firsthand that life can be complicated, sad, and lonely. I lived for many years in the depths of sorrow and unawareness. I failed to see beyond my turbulent circumstances, too afraid to dream, desire, and, at times, even hope.

Somewhere, somehow in the deep recesses of my being, I knew that there had to be an answer. The answer was within ME all along. I reclaimed my freedom when I discovered the power within—knowing that I can choose my role and behavior. In turn, the universe matched my thoughts and intentions and delivered with accuracy the desired manifestation.

At that time, I did not understand where all of my newfound resilience was coming from, nor cared. I knew that I had to listen to the voice inside, to make a move in a life-changing direction.

I searched for meaning and purpose. I asked the universe to provide clarity and a path to ultimate fulfillment and joy. It took years, and in small increments, my life changed for the better. I was once and for all director of my life's story.

I am now living a life that, at one time, was only a dream. I have a loving and supportive husband, a wonderful family, and trusted and caring friends. We have everything we need and want. I have a great life, and I continue to ask for more. More joy, happiness, health, and fun because that is what life is all about.

As a Jack Canfield Success Principles Trainer, an obsessive Abraham Hicks aficionado, and a student of all things LOA, I am excited to share what I have learned, studied, witnessed, and experienced. It does not have to take you years or months to learn how to create the life you want and deserve.

I challenge you to see life from a different perspective, one of hope, enthusiasm, and resilience. If I can do it, so can you.

Please understand that when we leverage the power of the Law of Attraction, we can face any problem, overcome any obstacle and enjoy ultimate success in everything we choose to do.

Our current beliefs influence how we view life and the world around us. Our definition of happiness and success is uniquely relevant to our desires based on past experiences and present circumstances.

Negative thinking permeates and has affected our sense of worth and self- esteem. Many believe that we must undergo pain to gain, that hard work is the secret to success, and that reward follows suffering.

These false, limiting beliefs have been the root cause of low achievement, frustration, chronic depression, addictions, illness, and overall unhappiness.

The success matrix changes as you move about your daily life, wishing for something more or different. And although innately, we all desire to be happy, our level of happiness is still a CHOICE. And it is the nature of that choice that this challenge is designed around.

This challenge will help you adjust your mindset and shed years of limiting beliefs to create the life you have always wanted.

"The world is

unfathomable

And so are we, and so is every being that exists in this world."

Carlos Castaneda-

WHAT CAN YOU EXPECT FROM THIS CHALLENGE:

- A process to help you clearly define your desires
- Discover what has been getting in the way of your success
- Learn to leverage the law of attraction in your favor
- Learn to prioritize your core values
- Think about your LIFE PURPOSE differently
- Learn how to overcome obstacles and make peace with the past.
- Learn skills and techniques to help you overcome bad habits, addictions, cravings, and temptations
- Develop your emotional intelligence and honor your feelings
- Learn to make focused decisions
- Gain confidence and self-esteem
- Learn to visualize and affirm for maximum manifestation results
- Learn to trust your instincts (built-in guidance system)
- Learn the best time to take action
- Unblock stubborn negative beliefs
- Establish a healthy balance in all areas of your life
- An easy-to-follow framework
- Short easy daily reads
- Simple but powerful daily challenges
- Find motivation and inspiration
- Maximum results IF you remain committed and consistent
- Recommended reading list for extra support

BE PREPARED

- Set aside at least thirty minutes
- Take as long as you can with each exercise. Contemplate the information, and your challenge answers
- Schedule a time when you are most likely to have privacy
- Find a quiet, comfortable spot and avoid any distractions
- Every day, preferably in the morning, write down four things you appreciate or love about: 1. Yourself, 2. Your family, 3. Your home, 4. Your job/career.

Now that you're ready, get started with Day 1!

CLEARLY DEFINE YOUR DESIRE
DAY-1

HOW DO YOU DEFINE HAPPINESS AND SUCCESS?

What does happiness mean to you? What is your definition of success? In what areas of your life do you wish for improvement or want to change? What would make your life easier and more enjoyable?

Is it to have a loving mate? A great relationship with your partner, children, parents, siblings, friends, and coworkers? Is it enjoyable, satisfying work?

Is it to have more fun, play, travel, or learn new things? A comfortable home and a car? Is it luxury and unlimited abundance? Is it peace, joy, happiness, passion, and excitement?

Is it stability, safety, security, and peace of mind? How about health and wellness? Is it confidence, self-esteem, and clarity? Is it all of the above and more? Do you know what you want?

Has anyone ever asked you that question? Have you ever felt guilty about desiring material things or circumstances you think you may not deserve?

EARLY CHILDHOOD PROGRAMMING

Consider that what we hear and experience as children goes deep into the subconscious and has a great impact on who we are as adults, which may explain some things.

Do any of the following statements possibly made by well-meaning adults, caregivers, or teachers ring true for you?

"You can't always have what you want."
"You only think about yourself."
"Money doesn't grow on trees."
"We can't afford that."
"Get your head out of the clouds."
"Don't eat that; you're getting fat."
"Eat everything on your plate."
"Stop talking."
"Don't be stupid."

The list goes on. It is no wonder that the adult mind contains no shortage of negative inner voices that keep us from reaching our goals or attaining our deepest desires. BUT, it doesn't have to be this way.

WHAT ARE YOUR GREATEST DESIRES?

What would it be if you could be, do, or have anything? What does your life look like when all your dreams come true? What are some of your deepest desires, and what do you daydream about? If you had a magic Genie that could grant you unlimited wishes, what would you ask?

CLARITY - CHANGE- GROWTH

When you begin to strip away layers of negative childhood programming, you become aware of your true identity and what you truly value. Your true development starts when you feel free to choose what type of person you would like to be, what circumstances you would like to create, and what difference you would like to make.

The progression of your character is up to you. What qualities do you wish to possess or enhance? If you were to die tomorrow, what would others remember you for? How do you wish to interact in the world, what contributions do you wish to make, and what type of mark do you want to leave behind?

Too many people live mundane, mediocre lives because they fail to ask themselves such questions.

- Dig deep inside and uncover what truly makes you happy.
- **When you give yourself permission to want and desire, that desire becomes clear and intentional.**
- Clarity and intent are necessary for the process of creation.
- **Please don't hold back; It is essential to want, desire, wish and daydream.**
- You can only have what is reflected in your imagination.

> "A CLEAR VISION BACKED BY DEFINITE PLANS, GIVES YOU A TREMENDOUS FEELING OF CONFIDENCE AND PERSONAL POWER."
>
> Brian Tracy-

Don't let your life be created by default; take the time to think about what makes you happy and what brings you joy and satisfaction.

CHALLENGE:

Write down everything you want to be, do, or have in the below seven areas of your life. Make this list as long as you want. Note: you must write in the present tense; more on this principle later, but for now, keep it in mind.

- Financial/Income/Debt Reduction/Investments/Net worth:
  Example: "I have perfect credit," "I have ten million dollars in my bank account."

- Business/ Career:
  Example: "I have a fun and satisfying business doing what I love." "I have my own business of buying and remodeling homes to sell."

- Fun /Recreation/Sports/Hobbies/Travel:
  Example: "I love traveling all over Europe; my favorite place, for now, is Greece."

- Health/Fitness:
  Example: "I am healthy, I feel great, and I love my well-defined body," "I have tons of energy and stamina."

- Relationships/Family/Friends
  Example: "My spouse and I have a loving and passionate relationship."

- Personal/Projects/Learning/Purchases
  Example: "I'm having fun learning Spanish." "I love it when I rock climb; it makes me feel alive."

- Community Service/Contributions/Legacy
  Example: "I am proud that I can donate lots of money to charity each year."

Challenge yourself to write as much as possible.
The universe does not understand vagueness; be crystal clear.

_____

_____

_____

_____

_____

_____

_____

_____

_____

_____

_____

_____

_____

_____

_____

_____

_____

_____

_____

_____

_____

_____

_____

_____

COMMON CONDITIONING

Many of us have been conditioned to blame the quality of our lives on someone else. It is easier to blame, complain, and make excuses rather than change the habits that keep us from taking responsibility.

Consider that our practiced behavior and habitual thought process have created specific neural pathways in our brain. These pathways are like record grooves, so when you think and behave a certain way over and over, the grooves become more profound and deeper-rooted habits.

After a while, the frequent practices become beliefs that seem automatic and out of your control.

The good news is that you **ARE** in control. The mind only does what you tell it to do. It is never independent of your instructions.

Scientists have found that when you think, feel, and act differently, the brain rewires itself.

You can change habits and beliefs because a belief is only a thought you keep thinking.

> TRAIN YOUR MIND AS HARD AS YOU WOULD TRAIN YOUR BODY

CHANGE THE THOUGHT, CHANGE THE HABIT, CHANGE THE BELIEF.

Knowing that you can rewire your brain to think on purpose gives you 100% responsibility for what shows up in your life, so there is no room for victimhood. Stop coming up with reasons why you can't and why you haven't up until now.

E+R= O
EVENT + RESPONSE = OUTCOME

Excuses and blaming, including yourself, will not change the past, but acknowledging and leveraging your mind power to create the future you want is something to get excited about.

Become aware of the range of choices that may be possible in any given circumstance.

The following formula will help you understand this.

Every outcome you experience in life results from how you <u>choose</u> to respond to an event. If you do not like what you are currently experiencing, you have two choices:

1. You CAN change your thinking; change the pictures you hold in your head.
2. You CAN change your behavior; how you communicate.

You CAN break out of your habitual response to circumstances and create new neural pathways in your brain. Many factors can contribute to the outcome, but they are not the deciding factor. For every excuse, there are many success stories of people who have faced similar circumstances but prevailed.

You can blame the (**Event**) for the **Outcome**, such as the alarm not going off, the weather, traffic, and so on, or; you can change your (**Response**) to the (**Events**) and get the (**Outcome**) you want.

THERE ARE THREE RESPONSES (R)
I HAVE CONTROL OVER
BEHAVIOR-THOUGHT -VISUAL IMAGERY

"THE KEY TO ACCEPTING RESPONSIBILITY FOR YOUR LIFE IS TO ACCEPT THE FACT THAT YOUR CHOICES, EVERYONE OF THEM, ARE LEADING YOU INEXORABLY EITHER TO SUCCESS OR FAILURE, HOWEVER YOU DEFINE THOSE TERMS."

NEIL BOOTS -

CHALLENGE:

PART 1: Pretend you have already taken a little more responsibility for several different areas in your life. Complete the following statements, writing in the <u>present tense.</u>

- I choose to take a little more responsibility for my life and well-being.
  Example: "I cook healthy meals, exercise, take vitamins."

- I choose to take a little more responsibility for attaining my goals.
  Example: "I'm taking classes and learning more about what I want to do for a living."

- I choose to take a little more responsibility for the success of my relationships.
  Example: "I listen when my partner is talking," "I call my family often."

- I choose to take a little more responsibility for the level of my self- esteem.
  Example: "I take care of my body by eating well and going for walks."

No one owes me anything. No one is responsible
for filling my life with happiness.
I do not blame my parents, bosses, friends, the
media, coworkers, clients, partners, weather,
economy, astrological chart, politicians, or past.
There is only one person responsible for the
quality of my life; **ME.**

_____

_____

_____

_____

_____

_____

_____

_____

_____

_____

_____

_____

_____

_____

_____

_____

_____

_____

_____

_____

_____

_____

TAKE RESPONSIBILITY -2
DAY-3

CHOOSE THE RESPONSE, CHANGE THE OUTCOME

The day you choose your responses is when your life will begin to get better. If you want something different, you have to start doing something different. For example, You are driving down the road to get to work. You listen to music and traffic flows; basically, you have a pretty good morning. Suddenly, brake lights ahead! It could be an accident, a stalled vehicle, road construction?

AT THIS JUNCTURE, YOU HAVE OPTIONS:

- You could choose to get angry, bang your fist on the steering wheel, roll your eyes, say a few curse words. You can have an internal dialogue with yourself about how the traffic in the area keeps getting worse, that people are stupid and that you will be late.

- You begin to worry about getting fired. Everything just turned into a nightmare, and the day is just getting started.

OR

- You can <u>choose</u> to keep calm and acknowledge that the event is out of your control. You have developed a habit of being prepared for such circumstances. You have stocked up your car with fun music and audiobooks, and you leave home with plenty of time to spare.

- You may even take advantage of the slow-moving traffic to look out the window and take in your surroundings. You have developed a patient attitude of appreciation for your car and the roads you drive on. Before you know it, you are moving again and resume your journey.

Same event with two different scenarios. Can you guess the outcome of both responses?

- In the first response, there was blaming, complaining, and making excuses;

- The second response showed responsibility.

Blaming is a very typical response when not taking 100% responsibility. Whom could you have blamed for the slowdown? And what good would that have done anyway?

I crafted the response- I took action- I thought the thought- I said what I said- I created the feeling- I took the job- I'm late for work- I abandoned my dream- I didn't say no- I said yes- I committed- I ignored my intuition- I chose him- I trusted her- I believed him- I ate the cake- I decided not to exercise- I didn't listen to my doctor.

Most people only complain about things they have chosen not to take action on. A complaint acknowledges you have a preference but choose not to pursue it.

For many, it's easier to complain, make excuses, and blame others than take personal responsibility and make the necessary changes.

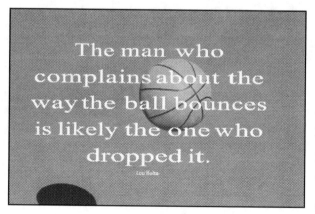

The man who complains about the way the ball bounces is likely the one who dropped it.

Successful people do the opposite of complaint; they take action even by taking risks.

For example, let's say you're at a restaurant and you're served cold food. You nicely ask the waiter to warm your food or give you another plate.

You offered a solution (you took action to rectify the situation). Do you think that taking action may be too risky? Most people would rather complain and blame than risk failure, confrontation, ridicule, and judgment.

A COMPLAINT WITHOUT A SOLUTION IS EMPTY AND WORTHLESS SO, STOP COMPLAINING ABOUT WHAT YOU'RE NOT WILLING TO CHANGE

CHALLENGE:

Make two columns. In the first column, write a list of your most common complaints. In the second column, write down the possible solution.

It is up to you to come up with alternatives. Thinking through the possible problems is the first step; the second is to develop workable solutions. Put your thinking cap on and make it a good list.

MY MOST COMMON COMPLAINTS

I'm always stuck in traffic!

MY SOLUTION

I set my alarm and leave my home early.

BONUS CHALLENGE

Spend one entire day without complaining, blaming, or making excuses, and note what happens.

_____

_____

_____

_____

_____

_____

_____

_____

_____

_____

_____

_____

_____

_____

_____

_____

_____

_____

_____

_____

_____

_____

_____

TAKE RESPONSIBILITY -3

DAY-4

ASK FOR FEEDBACK

You have spent three days on responsibility because it requires you to be aware, dedicated, and disciplined, although it is a simple principle. Taking full responsibility does not mean going at it alone. Support and feedback are precious, so ask.

Others may see things about us that we don't see. Your insecurities or stubborn tendencies may blind you, but there is the truth, and unless you know it, you cannot make changes.

Your life will also give you feedback. How has your behavior affected you? Is your current life situation reflective of what you truly desire? You either have what you want, or you don't; you are happy, or you're not, so take feedback with an open mind and with appreciation.

THE PROMISE TO YOURSELF

Committing to this challenge is a promise to yourself, and it is the first step in creating the life you want and deserve.

Your intention is powerful, but it requires consistency, dedication, persistence, and patience.

There may be times when you're tempted to put the day's challenge off, but don't! You must maintain the schedule.

Developing good routines, following through, and creating positive momentum is part of the process. Your success with this program is ultimately up to you.

HERE ARE SOME CRUCIAL STEPS TO HELP YOU STAY ON TRACK:

SET A SCHEDULE:
- Make time for this challenge by scheduling a consistent time and a place without distractions.

- Set a daily reminder on your phone or calendar and place reminders around your home for extra motivation.

KEEP TRACK:

- Keep track of your progress. Every time you see yourself moving forward, you gain the motivation to reach your goal.

REWARD YOURSELF:

- Rewarding yourself with something fun, uplifting, and in line with your overall goals is essential.

ACCOUNTABILITY PARTNER:

- Consider asking someone you trust to schedule a call every few days or once a week to share your progress.

SET BOUNDARIES:

- Setting boundaries with other commitments and relationships may be difficult at first, but necessary.

- Be aware of toxic people and distractions.

- Make it clear to others around you that you are serious and committed to this process, and surround yourself with understanding, supportive people.

BE PATIENT:

- Understand that this is a thirty-one-day process, and remind yourself of the short and long-term benefits.

- You have already taken the most significant step; starting; keep going; you got this!

> Focus and keep your eyes on your goals. Do not let your attention drift into sameness, mediocre or negative existence. You are better than that; you are a powerful creator.

CHALLENGE:

Please write down the statements below and read them aloud to yourself three times.

- **I am in charge of my thoughts.**

- I am in charge of my words.

- **I am in charge of the images in my head.**

- I am in charge of my feelings.

- **I am responsible for my choice of music, movies, and books.**

- I choose the people I spend time with, the conversations I engage in, the activities I pursue, and the behavior I tolerate.

- **Everything that I experience, both internally and externally, is the result of my choices.**

KEEP UP WITH YOUR APPRECIATION JOURNAL

THE LAW OF ATTRACTION-1

DAY-5

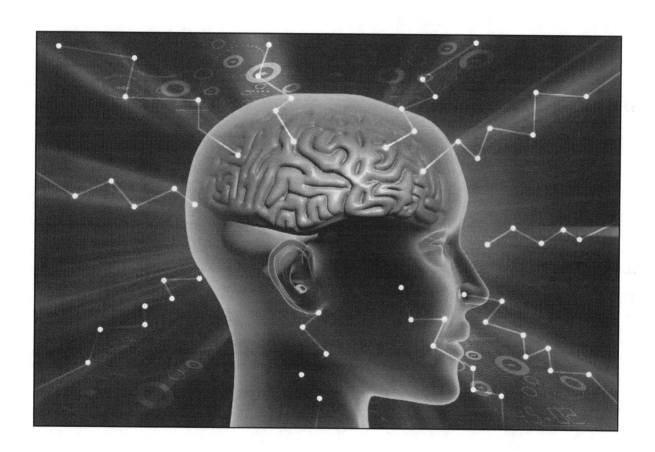

YOU GET WHAT YOU THINK ABOUT

Simply put, "The Law of Attraction" is "that which is like unto itself is drawn." (Abraham Hicks) Or "like, attracts like." Thoughts are magnetized, so you get more of what you habitually think about.

Have you ever said or heard someone say, "you reap what you sow," "what goes around comes around," "It's Karma"?

> "every action has an equal and opposite reaction."
>
> -Isaac Newton-

These common sayings are right on target; what we think about, imagine, and visualize will materialize IF there is a focus or habit to propel it.

Be wise and pay attention to what sort of things you're choosing to focus on. Please don't make it a habit to think, talk, and imagine something you don't wish to see or experience.

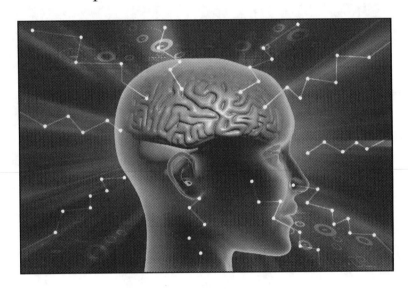

It is interesting that Ancient philosophers, scientists, and religious leaders also referenced and taught the "law of attraction," individuals such as Plato, Socrates, The Buddha, and Jesus.

Great thinkers, mathematicians, and poets such as Shakespeare, Blake, Emerson, Newton, Einstein, and Beethoven conveyed "the law of attraction" in their famous works.

Modern successful individuals have also discovered the secret to success

and have shared the formula in books and talks. In 1937 an American author, Napoleon Hill, wrote one of the top self-help books in modern history, Think and Grow Rich. He believed that expectation is key to having everything you want.

Whether or not they understand the formula, successful people apply it in one way, shape, or form.

ENERGY AND VIBRATION

How do thoughts manifest? Everything is energy, made up of tiny particles that vibrate at specific frequencies. This energy can be seen in

modern EKG Electrocardiography (ECG or EKG[a]), the process of recording the electrical activity of the heart and brain.

And, like a magnet, our thoughts have an invisible force that attracts other thoughts to match.

So, reality is a series of thoughts that gathered momentum and attracted their match until a manifestation occurred.

OUR THOUGHTS EMIT ENERGY THAT VIBRATES AT SPECIFIC FREQUENCIES. WHEN YOU HAVE NEGATIVE THOUGHTS, YOUR MIND AND BODY EMIT NEGATIVE FREQUENCIES. WHEN YOU THINK POSITIVE THOUGHTS, YOUR MIND EMITS POSITIVE FREQUENCIES.

When you are negative, you attract negativity, and when you are positive, you attract positivity; it is that simple.

"The Law of attraction" will be referenced often throughout the material, for it is the foundation and the reason why the principles laid out in this workbook are effective.

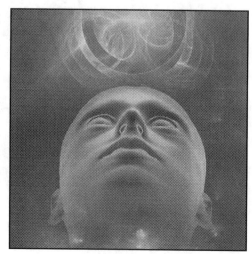

DR. EMOTO'S WATER EXPERIMENTS

Dr. Emoto is a Japanese scientist who discovered that exposing water to thoughts, written messages, music, and specific names caused water from the same source to change its molecular structure.

Positivity caused the water to change into crystals with increased light, while negativity caused the water to become unorganized shapes with less light.

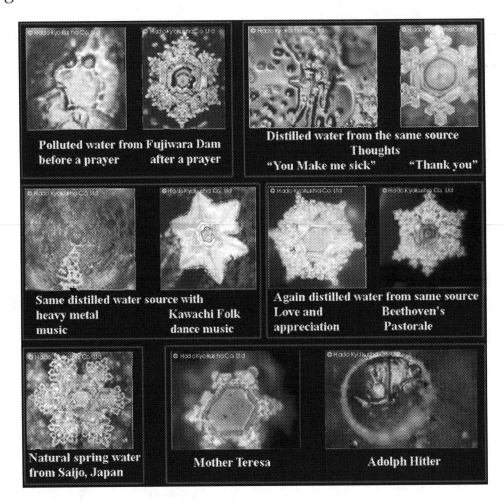

Polluted water from Fujiwara Dam before a prayer   after a prayer

Distilled water from the same source
Thoughts
"You Make me sick"   "Thank you"

Same distilled water source with heavy metal music   Kawachi Folk dance music

Again distilled water from same source
Love and appreciation   Beethoven's Pastorale

Natural spring water from Saijo, Japan

Mother Teresa

Adolph Hitler

If thoughts can change water's crystallized shapes, imagine how thoughts can change our cells' structure, over 60% percent water. Watch: https://www.youtube.com/watch?v=tAvzsjcBtx8

THE RICE EXPERIMENT

1. Place 1 cup of cooked rice into three separate containers. Place a lid on each.
2. Mark the containers, one with a positive phrase such as "Thank You," or "I love you," the other with "stupid," or "I hate you," and simply ignore the third.
3. Place the containers 12 inches apart.
4. At least once a day, talk to the rice containers with emotion.

For example: Say to one rice container, "You stupid rice, I hate you," say it with anger, then say, "thank you, rice, I love you" to the other container with an attitude of appreciation and ignore the third container.

After about twenty days of consistently saying the above words to the rice, the rice in the positive comments container will remain nice and clean. The container you addressed negatively and with contempt will have begun to rot, and the third ignored container will have normal decay.

TRY THIS EXPERIMENT AND THEN IMAGINE WHAT
YOUR WORDS, THOUGHTS, AND INTENTIONS
ARE DOING TO YOU AND HOW YOU INFLUENCE
OTHERS AND THE WORLD AROUND YOU.

CHALLENGE:

What are you attracting? What are the subjects that occupy your mind most of the time? Take an honest inventory of what you usually focus on, talk about, read, etc., by writing a list.

EXAMPLE:

- I usually read books that contain lots of sad and depressing stories.

- **Some of the video games I play are very graphic and violent.**

- I usually talk about how unhappy I am at my job.

- **I want to think good thoughts, but I always want to be prepared by thinking about what could go wrong.**

- Some of my friends are always complaining, and I end up joining in.

After you write your list, follow it up by writing about how you can think or do something different about the subject.

EXAMPLE:

- I choose to read positive books.

- **I am going to reevaluate my choice of video games.**

- I only talk about what I like about my job.

- **I think about what can go right instead of what can go wrong.**

- When my friends begin their usual complaining, I will steer the conversation in a positive direction.

THE LAW OF ATTRACTION -2
DAY-6

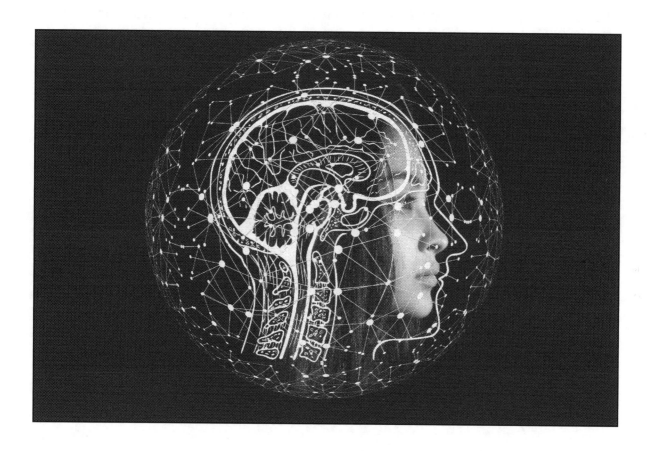

THE POWERFUL CREATIVE FORMULA

The Law of Attraction has three necessary components that are easy to understand; ASK, ALLOW, and RECEIVE.

ASK

The first part of the process is automatic; you ask by thinking. When you think about something you like or want, you automatically request the universe for more of the same. When you think about something you do not want, you also ask for more of the same.

The universe is inclusive and does not hear the word NO. You will eventually manifest what you habitually think about, whether you want it or not. For example, if you think, "I don't want to be late for work," the universe does not hear the word "don't," it only hears "late for work." A better thought or statement would be, "I will be at work on time." Thoughts emit vibrational signals at particular frequencies, so, like a magnet, the Law of Attraction always attracts its equivalent frequency.

This process is not instantaneous for apparent reasons, but thoughts manifest eventually, so pay attention to what you are thinking and how you express those thoughts to get what you want.

Unless you are brain dead, you are always in a state of asking.

ALLOW

When your thoughts generate feelings and emotions, you allow the attraction process. Your feelings are consistently and reliably alerting you to upcoming manifestations. If you feel good positive emotions such as happiness, hopefulness, and excitement, you are on your way to manifesting a positive outcome.

If you feel down, angry, depressed, or annoyed, you are on the road to manifesting a negative outcome. Pay attention to what you're feeling and what your emotions tell you. Do more, think more, and talk more about it if it feels good. If it does not feel good, then pivot to thoughts that feel better.

Pivoting to better feeling thoughts may be challenging, depending on how much momentum the original idea had to begin with. If you catch the negative thought quickly, pivoting is easy.

Do not worry and make a big deal about not being able to pivot quickly; getting down on yourself for having negative thoughts only reinforces the negative feeling and adds to the negative momentum.

The process of pivoting is often the first step at the beginning of shifting your vibration. This process helps you to clearly define your desire

Instead, realize that it is necessary to have a certain level of negative (contrast) in your life, for, without contrast, you would never know what you prefer. The key is to acknowledge your preference quickly, adjust your thoughts and focus on what you prefer.

The best time to begin the process of purposely ASKING is just before going to sleep at night and as soon as you wake up in the morning.

Intend to wake up happy and determined to have a good day. In the morning, repeat that intention. Practice those intentions, and you will notice yourself enjoying a good night's sleep and waking up refreshed and energized.

RECEIVE

The process of receiving manifestations is also automatic. Your only job is to ALLOW. Once you begin to think on purpose and with intent, you create habitual thought patterns followed by physical manifestations.

Example: your alarm goes off and wakes you up, and you think, "I'm so tired, I don't

want to get up yet." Thoughts of being tired and not having enough sleep cause you to ASK for more sleep; (automatic).

- If you choose to focus on how tired and sleepy you are, you will begin to ALLOW negative momentum towards RECEIVING more sleepy feelings leading to crankiness and disappointment.

- Instead, you choose to appreciate the alarm that keeps you from running late. You acknowledge that you do not like feeling sleepy and tired and think about a solution; (perhaps going to bed earlier); you feel appreciation and in control.

Because you focused on the solution rather than the problem, you naturally ALLOW and RECEIVE more sleep and energy in the future.

WILL APPRECIATING MY CURRENT SITUATION CAUSE ME TO HAVE MORE OF THE SAME UNWANTED PROBLEM?

No, finding things to appreciate in your current situation does not keep you in that situation if that situation is not what you want. Intentionally focusing on what is good about your current situation helps raise the overall vibration, which puts you in a positive state of manifesting what you DO want.

It seems simple enough; think positive thoughts and get what you want! So why do most people find this challenging? Why does it seem more natural to think negatively, complain, and blame? Why does it sometimes feel like our thoughts are thinking and controlling us?

Remember that your current thinking pattern has developed over time; switching gears can be challenging. Habits formed must be reprogrammed. With practice, you can reprogram your mind to build new thought patterns.

By purposely keeping your mind busy with positive, wanted thoughts, you will soon witness good habits naturally and effortlessly forming and things and circumstances that you've been wanting manifesting.

Try this, when you notice yourself thinking negative thoughts, ask yourself, "what am I getting ready to create?", "What is it that I want?" "What is the opposite of that negative thought?" "What is the solution to the problem?" By asking yourself these questions and then focusing on the answers, you take control of your thoughts.

Positive Energy = High Frequency Vibration	**Ask** Thinking is asking. Whether it's something wanted or unwanted.	Negative Energy = Low Frequency Vibration
Appreciating, loving, giving complementing, enjoying, savoring, welcoming, cheering, celebrating, generosity, caring, attentive, loyal, thoughtful, considerate, kind, caring, amiable, faithful, devoted	**Allow** Our feelings and emotions indicate what we are allowing	Criticizing, complaining blaming, condemning, regretting, arguing, fighting resenting, accusing, protesting, whining, belly aching, gossiping
Beliefs Possible, certain		**Beliefs** Impossible, uncertain
Emotions/Feelings Joy, appreciation, happiness, empowerment, freedom, love, passion, zeal enthusiasm, eagerness, earnestness, optimism, confidence, contentment	**Receive** We eventually manifest what we ask for and allow, whether we like it or not	**Emotions/Feelings** Insecurity, guilt, unworthiness, fear, grief, despair, depression, powerlessness, anger, revenge, hatred, rage, jealousy, worry, blame, discouragement, disappointment, doubt, overwhelment, impatience, frustration,

CHALLENGE:

Write down some of your most common negative thoughts, and then use the formula below to change them to positives.

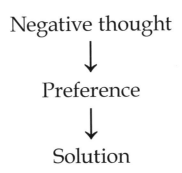

Negative thought

↓

Preference

↓

Solution

EXAMPLE: Let us say that you developed the habit of being down on yourself over time because of unwanted and unhealthy pounds. When negative thoughts such as :

"I'm disgusted with the way I look; I'm weak and have no self-control."

Replace:

- Preference; (What you want and why you want it)- "I want to be healthy because I want to feel good in my body.

- Solution (What will it take to make this happen) - "I will do some research on the best way to start a healthy eating and exercise routine." Now make it a present tense, positive statement. "I appreciate my healthy body and how quickly things are changing."

MIND & BODY CONNECTION -1
DAY-7

AN AMAZING TAG TEAM

Modern medicine has largely dismissed the correlation between the mind and the body since the late 14th early 16th centuries. During that time, a human body could only be dissected and studied with the Pope's permission because such a procedure was considered blasphemy. The Pope only gave his consent if the physical body was studied separately from the mind. The church had considerable power and believed that the study of emotions might tread on followers' faith, potentially threatening that power.

During the the1960's, Eastern philosophies began challenging Western thinking on the connection between mind and body. Since then, alternative therapies for treating physical and mental illness have begun to be applied. Acupuncture has been used for centuries to perform invasive surgeries without anesthesia!

Mind and body connections have gained momentum, including alternative therapies such as Massage, Acupuncture, Holistic Medicine, Applied Kinesiology, also known as muscle- testing, and EFT (Emotional Freedom Technique), to name a few.

It is interesting that Ancient philosophers, scientists, and religious leaders also referenced and taught the "law of attraction," individuals such as Plato,

Socrates, The Buddha, and Jesus. Great thinkers, mathematicians, and poets such as Shakespeare, Blake, Emerson, Newton, Einstein, and Beethoven conveyed "the law of attraction" in their famous works. Modern successful individuals have also discovered the secret to success and have shared the formula in books and talks. In 1937 an American author, Napoleon Hill, wrote one of the top self-help books in modern history, Think and Grow

Rich. He believed that expectation is key to having everything you want. Whether or not they understand the formula, successful people apply it in one way, shape, or form.

APPLIED KINESIOLOGY

Applied Kinesiology, also known as muscle testing, is a method of diagnosis. It is a treatment based on the belief that various muscles are linked to particular organs and glands.

Specific muscle weakness can signal internal problems such as nerve damage, reduced blood supply, chemical imbalances, or other organ or gland problems.

Correcting this muscle weakness can help heal a problem in the associated organ.

The technique is also helpful in exploring the relationship of one's thoughts to one's physiological strength. When you negatively talk to yourself, you weaken your body's physiology. Negative thinking harms your physical and mental health.

EFT, EMOTIONAL FREEDOM TECHNIQUE

The Emotional Freedom Technique, also known as tapping, is based on ancient acupressure and modern psychology principles. Tapping targets specific meridian endpoints while focusing on the negative emotion or physical sensation, calming the nervous system to restore energy balance, and rewiring the brain to respond in healthy ways by tapping the meridian points with your fingers.

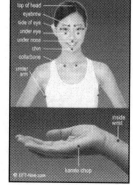

This technique has helped in insomnia, chronic fatigue, headaches, muscle tension, body aches, and much more.

Note: These techniques, although highly effective, are suggested supplemental therapies. Please continue to get regular checkups with your physician and do your research. www. thetappingsolution.com

CELLS AND BIOLOGY

In his book "The Biology of Belief," former medical school professor and research scientist Bruce H. Lipton, Ph.D., writes about research experiments performed by himself and other scientists that examine how our cells receive and process information.

The research shows that genes and DNA do not control our biology; instead, DNA is controlled by signals outside the cell, including energetic messages from our positive and negative thoughts. The amazing research in cell biology and quantum physics shows that we can retrain our thinking and change our bodies.

Have you ever been driving, and suddenly from the corner of your eye, you see another car getting too close, and you automatically feel a tingling sensation in your body? Or have you ever been embarrassed and felt your body temperature rise, your cheeks flush, and your palms perspire? Maybe you have felt shocked over some horrible news and felt your stomach flip and your knees weaken?

Have you ever felt butterflies in your stomach just before an important event, a speech, or an important meeting? Have you ever succumbed to the power of suggestion and yawned because you observed someone else yawning?

If your answer is yes to any of the questions above, you have felt your body's reaction to an event that began outside our body, a thought, or an observation; you have experienced the mind and body connection.

"The words we use are more than just words, they literally are having a biological influence in our bodies, they're changing the way our genes in our DNA are being upregulated or downregulated for our health and wellbeing."

Greg Braden-

Recommended Documentary: Heal, a Netflix Original.

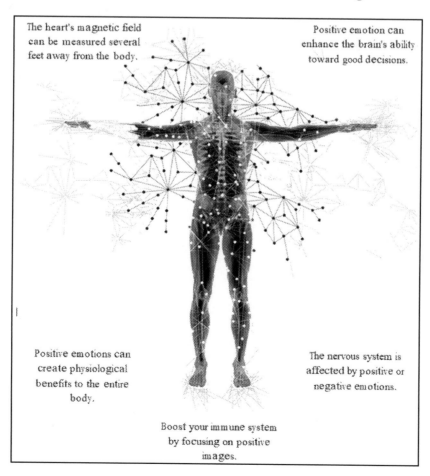

The heart's magnetic field can be measured several feet away from the body.

Positive emotion can enhance the brain's ability toward good decisions.

Positive emotions can create physiological benefits to the entire body.

The nervous system is affected by positive or negative emotions.

Boost your immune system by focusing on positive images.

CHALLENGE:

Write down a list of your everyday stress triggers along with some possible solutions.

EXAMPLE:

Stress Trigger: Making a flight on time.

Solution: I will check in as soon as possible (most airlines will allow online check-in 24 hours before departure). I will write a packing checklist and pack my bags the night before. I will set my alarm, get a good night's rest, and leave with plenty of spare time.

DON'T RUSH THROUGH THIS PROCESS; GIVE IT SOME THOUGHT AND COME UP WITH GREAT ALTERNATIVES AND SOLUTIONS YOU WILL IMPLEMENT RIGHT AWAY.

MIND & BODY CONNECTION -2
DAY-8

THE PERFECT TAG TEAM

THE CONSCIOUS MIND

The conscious mind receives outside information and stimuli through the five senses, then it begins to analyze the data and makes decisions. It can only deal with one thought at a time, and it has no memory.

The conscious mind is the reality in which we physically sense the world around us. It is the physical reality of seeing, feeling, tasting, smelling, and hearing. The conscious mind feeds the subconscious information.

THE SUBCONSCIOUS MIND

The subconscious mind is very complex, and it is what controls our bodily functions such as breathing, digestion, and heart rate. The subconscious records every event we have ever lived and the accompanying emotions.

The subconscious receives our invaluable direction through our intuition and impulses, bringing us ideas, insights, and solutions to our everyday dilemmas and desires.

CONSCIOUS AND SUBCONSCIOUS TAG TEAM

Your conscious mind receives your intentions through outside stimuli. In turn, your subconscious processes the information matching it with emotion, and eventually becomes a physical manifestation.

The subconscious will create whatever the conscious mind feeds it, so you must pay attention to what you choose to think about, talk about, read about, listen to, and choose to see, especially when reinforced by strong feelings and emotions.

THE SUBCONSCIOUS IS WHERE BELIEFS AND HABITS ARE FORMED.

If things are not going right in your life, you must reevaluate what you are feeding your consciousness and subsequently settle in your subconscious.

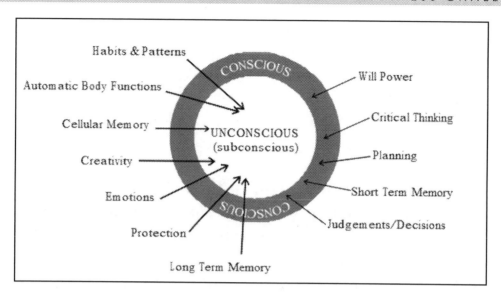

YOUR INNER BEING

Understanding the more significant part of yourself is to experience real power and freedom. Acknowledging your inner being brings you peace once you realize that you are not alone. Some people call it the soul, spirit, universe, or god.

It is who you were before you were born and who you will continue to be once you leave your physical body. The greater part of you is a constant companion that gives you feedback and direction but never judges.

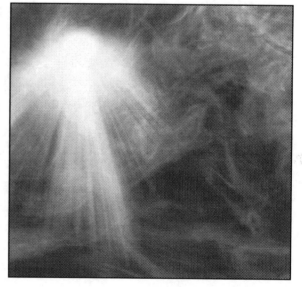

Your inner being takes real-time notes of all of your preferences, dreams, and desires, it never forgets, and it attempts to guide you toward those desires to the extent that you allow it.

When you feel good, you are in the state of allowing, and your inner being directs you toward your desires. Your inner being or higher- self is an integral part of your existence, working with you to create and help expand the universe.

You do not have to understand nor be an expert on the human mind to create. By default, most people create, react, and live a conditional life that brings little or no satisfaction.

By understanding the general creative process, you will appreciate the power of choice. Successful, powerful creators are proactive; they set the tone by choosing the thoughts that bring on the emotions that produce physical equivalence. Either way, in or out of alignment, the universe's laws are constant and consistent; you will manifest what you habitually think.

Make it a point, a habit, align yourself with your inner being, feel that solid relationship every day, and see how quickly and richly your life will change.

CHALLENGE:

Write down 20 things or more you appreciate about yourself and why. The WHY is particularly important in this exercise; take your time.

Note: For some, this exercise may feel awkward at first. Do not be hard on yourself if you cannot think of twenty things.

As you move along in the process of daily appreciation, this will change. Your self-esteem and confidence will grow, and so will your list.

🖋 Suggested Reading:

- Abraham Hicks (The Law of Attraction).
- Mind Powers, by John Kehoe.
- The Biology of Belief, by Bruce H. Lipton, PH.D.

THE ART OF APPRECIATION

DAY-9

HAVE YOU NOTICED?

Most people find it easier to complain and focus on what's going wrong instead of what's going right. If you pay close attention to people's conversations, it is clear negativity dominates, and pessimism, cynicism, and doubt abounds. For many people, most of their discussions include a "but."

"I agree, it is a nice day BUT, it won't last"

It takes exceptional awareness to begin and sustain good, upbuilding conversations that reflect appreciation.

CHOOSING HIGH-FREQUENCY WORDS

Appreciation and love are on the highest vibrational frequencies you could experience. Nothing connects you quicker and easier to your inner being than being in a state of appreciation and or love.

When you appreciate, you agree with what your inner being thinks about the subject, for your inner being is pure positive energy, always in appreciation, and is love.

Since the law of attraction will match you with whatever you are a vibrational match to, it is wise to practice the art of appreciation.

Appreciation v/s Gratitude What's the Difference?

It is common for people to use the words "appreciation" and "gratitude" interchangeably, so why is it encouraged to use the word appreciation instead of grateful in the Teachings of Abraham Hicks?

The words appreciation and gratefulness are on different vibrational frequencies, appreciation being higher and more powerful.

Being grateful implies overcoming a problem for which you feel gratitude, but the problem is the primary and dominant vibration.

Appreciation means to increase the value of; equivalent to the vibration of love and has no resistance. It is a similar difference between inspiration and motivation. Being inspired is being called to something; motivation means making yourself do something.

It may seem like splitting hairs, but words are important because humans have assigned meaning to words, and words conjure up emotions that turn into manifestations.

For example, "I'm grateful for my new job." The vibration is centered around overcoming the struggle, problem, or issue. On the other hand, "I appreciate my new job" focuses on the increased value of having a new job.

APPRECIATION JOURNAL

It would be best if you had written in your appreciation journal nine times by now. Are you noticing the difference this simple but powerful exercise can make?

Here are some tips for a satisfying and lasting appreciation journal writing experience.

FULLY COMMIT

There are varied opinions on journal writing frequency. Some suggest writing every day, others a couple of times a week.

I recommend making it part of your daily routine, at least for the first month. This process aims to make appreciation a habit, such as brushing your teeth.

WRITE WITH EMOTION

Consider sometimes going in-depth and more descriptive. Translating thought into language deepens the emotion, especially when coupled with visualization, all necessary components for speedy manifestations.

MAKE IT SPECIAL

Although unnecessary, obtaining a special notebook, journal, and pen specifically for journaling can enhance the experience. Set a time and a quiet place with minimum distractions.

FIND YOUR STYLE

Depending on your lifestyle and schedule, choose what works best for you, keeping in mind that it takes practice and consistency like any new habit.

CHALLENGE:

If you have not done so already, prepare a journal/notebook. Write at least four things you appreciate:

1. About Yourself
2. About Family and friends
3. About Your home and surroundings
4. About Your job/career

Look for things to appreciate as you go about your day—for example, nature, construction for road improvements, friendly, courteous people, etc.

Practice saying the words appreciation and love aloud and catch yourself when you use grateful instead and notice the subtle frequency difference.

EXAMPLE:

- I love waking up rested and refreshed.

- I appreciate my bed, sheets, and pillow; I love how they feel on my skin.

- I love that my morning unfolds flawlessly, helping me feel productive. I appreciate the rain, it cleans the atmosphere, and it smells so good. I love my hair; it is healthy and shiny; I feel proud.

LIVING WITH PURPOSE

DAY-10

LIVING WITH PURPOSE

Living with purpose means living with intention. It does not mean there is one thing that you should be doing or are responsible for. Living with purpose means injecting passion and determination into every activity you undertake and identifying the key things that bring you joy.

When you live with purpose, everything falls into place. You do what you love, what you are good at, and what is important.

With your desires clearly identified, you have a basis for making major life decisions. You deliberately pursue activities and goals that help you fulfill your dreams while naturally attracting people, resources, and opportunities. It means facing life with resilience, full power, and being present.

When you live with PURPOSE, you find your center, no longer being torn in every direction, losing focus, or easily distracted. Purposeful people have a direction in which all signs face.

WHEN YOU FIND YOUR PASSION, PURPOSE WILL FOLLOW

Passion is a strong emotion; it is what you consistently think about, obsess about, and dream about. It is investment and devotion to something or someone.

Passion is all-encompassing and denotes a natural high. Without passion, boredom sets in, and the inner fire burns out, leaving you depleted and prone to giving up.

Experiencing passion may be difficult to pinpoint because many of us have buried our passions under the weight of everyday living. Still, figuring out what you are passionate about will help you clarify and direct you toward a purpose.

WHAT IS YOUR DEFINITION OF SUCCESS?

Everyone's definition of success is different and can only be measured by you, so comparing yourself or being envious of someone else will only get in your way to living with purpose.

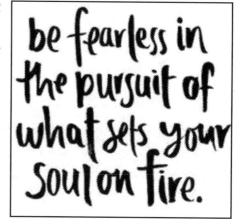

If your passion is teaching and you make teaching your career, you live with purpose, which is a success. If you desire to have a loving, healthy relationship with your spouse and have that, that is a success.

If you build a multi-million dollar company and find satisfaction in its everyday workings, you have found success. No matter what you are doing, if it is with passion, joy, and happiness, you are a success, and you live with purpose!

Don't let others weaken or suppress your voice. Choose to be all you want and can be without settling. Making yourself the priority is the most extraordinary form of self-sufficiency.

There are some key elements to living a happy and fulfilled life. Studies have shown that successful people have all three success elements present in their life. The goal is to recognize, identify, and commit to living your top passions.

Do not get bogged down with trying to figure out how you will reach your desires; the "Law of Attraction" will ensure you get there. Your only job is to allow your desires to manifest by recognizing when you are in the receiving mode (feeling good). Your part in the creation process is to be happy by living with intent.

MY APPROACH TO LIVING WITH PURPOSE HAS
ALWAYS BEEN TO CREATE THE LIFE I WANT,
ONE CONSCIOUS DECISION AT A TIME.

Oprah, Winfrey

Be aware that negative contrast will serve its purpose by helping you focus. Negative feelings will alert you when veering off your path so that you may regroup, recoup, and adjust.

A willingness to learn and grow is essential. Questions to ask yourself several times a day are "How am I feeling right now?", "What am I getting ready to attract?".

You are a powerful and successful creator, so start living your life on your terms, with passion and purpose.

THREE KEY ELEMENTS TO REMEMBER

CLARITY

Remember, vague dreams produce vague, scattered results.

BELIEF

Believe that anything is possible and believe in yourself.

DETERMINATION

Be stubborn about living with purpose. See obstacles as opportunities to adjust and grow. Be flexible and patient, but do not be deterred.

CHALLENGE:

Step 1

Make a list of 10 things that will make your life and work ideal. Please list them by order of importance. With these accomplished, you will feel you have reached success.

Step 2

Write at least a paragraph for each of the top 5 on your list. Describe what your life looks like while fully living that passion. Be as descriptive as possible, using enjoying, relaxing, and loving words. Make sure you write in the present tense.

EXAMPLE:

I am a famous writer and author.

As a successful writer and author, I make an excellent living by doing what I love every day. I enjoy using my imagination and bringing characters to life in a fun, dramatic scenes. It brings me great satisfaction to know that others love my books. One of my favorite things to do is travel the world for book signings because I love connecting with my fans face to face.

FACE WHAT ISN'T WORKING

DAY-11

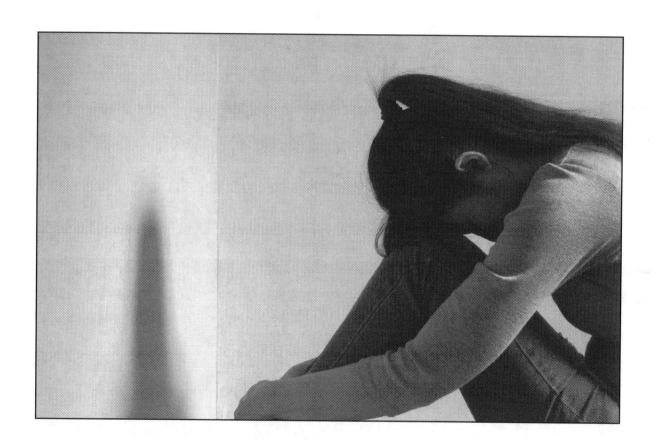

IT TAKES COURAGE TO FACE THE FACTS

Facing what is not working and hindering your ultimate success may be challenging but necessary. You must stop making excuses and denying yourself the life you truly want.

Stop defending where you are if where you are is not where you want to be. Victory and freedom are a reward for courage.

DO YOU PUT UP WITH, AVOID IT, JUSTIFY IT, CONCEAL IT, LIE ABOUT, OR DENY IT?

You cannot change what you cannot face, so you must be very honest with yourself; this requires deep and serious contemplation.

It would be helpful to look back on your list of what you want. Begin moving forward by acknowledging that what has kept you back is YOURSELF.

For example, you wish to be debt-free, write down all the reasons you have not been able to. Look to see where you can take steps to become debt-free.

Maybe it is to focus on just one debt at a time, perhaps a loan from a friend or a relative that you have not paid back yet. Make arrangements to pay it in payments that you can handle.

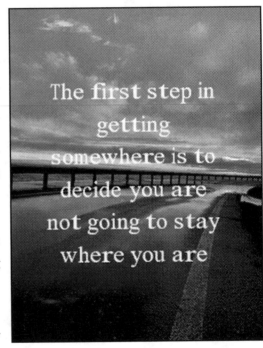

The **first step** in getting somewhere is to decide you are not going to stay where you are

Once you begin the new arrangements, you will start to feel relief from the stress of defaulting on your agreements.

Once you have paid the debt, you will feel great about it, and feeling great about money will only attract more money.

It's an easy process once you get started, and it will help you advance in all areas of your life.

The following challenge will be incredibly useful if you:

- Face the real reasons why you have or have not done something.

- Forgive yourself for not doing this sooner or not following through in the past. Start fresh, right here, right now.

- Come up with solutions that you can immediately implement.

- Please start with the right mindset and set the intention for improvement by writing it down.

- Witness the power of the "Law of Attraction" once you begin with the small steps and quickly gain momentum.

CHALLENGE:

1. Write a list of what is not working in your life. Maybe things you have wanted to change but have been afraid to face and avoid instead.
2. Write down some possible solutions, small steps you can take right away.

EXAMPLE: "What isn't working in my life is that I lack energy and motivation to move more. I know I need to exercise, but I get lazy and find excuses".

Solution:

"I go to bed a little earlier and wake up with energy. I go for a walk around my neighborhood every day". (write in present tense)

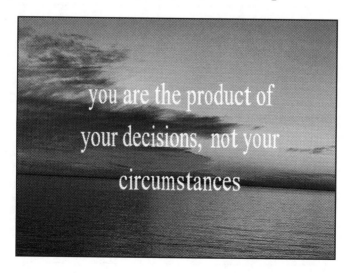

OVERCOMING BAD HABITS & ADDICTIONS

DAY-12

GETTING REAL

Do you have weaknesses that are undermining your good intentions? Or do you have some deep-rooted habits and addictions that are keeping you stuck? We all have them to various degrees.

Some habits may be minor such as nail-biting, exercising routines, or taking the same route to work. Daily routines are habits, and for a good reason, the brain is a multitasking genius, so forming habits allows it to go on autopilot and save energy.

Physical dependencies such as food and water are needed for survival, but other dependencies can be detrimental such as caffeine, sugar, nicotine, alcohol, and drugs, over the counter, and otherwise.

There are other addictions such as work, exercise, sex, porn, or gambling, not to mention compulsive behaviors. Some annoying habits may seem inconsequential, but some are not.

Suppose an outside substance or activity controls your mood and your life. If you cannot seem to live without it and even go as far as to have physical withdrawal from it, then there is a problem, and you must first get real with yourself and face it.

> If you defend the habits, then you don't have any intention of breaking them

FROM BAD TO GOOD

Our brains work on a trigger and reward basis. When we feel bad, disappointed, stressed, or depressed, we may reach for a quick temporary

fix such as alcohol, drugs, food, or other activity or substances to temporarily numb the pain and get relief.

That which has provided temporary relief is the powerful "feel good" hormone called dopamine. Feeling good is natural and desired; falling into a routine of bad habits to get a quick dose of dopamine can make putting an end to bad habits difficult.

Have you ever wondered why one potato chip isn't enough? Consider that around 70 percent of processed foods contain added sugar. Sugar is a feel- good substance that triggers dopamine release, and companies have taken advantage of the addictive nature of sugar so that you will continue to crave and buy their product.

FEAR

Some habits are formed because we fear facing the consequences of our actions or hiding negative experiences or problems. Temporary activities or substances also keep you from avoiding change and keep you going back for more.

To make changes is to tread in the unknown, that scary place of uncertainty. Many people stay in toxic relationships, bad jobs, undesirable locations, or do not make personal physical changes because of fear.

Habits become a crutch, and people feel lost and incapable without them. But, at what cost? Fear can be paralyzing, and thus reaching for something, anything, gives us temporary power and control, or so you think.

SECURITY

Habits form out of the need to feel safe and secure. We have a predictable outcome that spells security when we repeat a process.

Establishing healthy habits also provides us with safety, security, and dopamine!

ARE ADDICTIONS GENETICALLY PREDISPOSED?

Dr. Bruce H. Lipton Ph.D., a Development Biologist who wrote various books on cell biology, has the following to say about addiction:

"The addiction is not an illness. It's not a physical, organic thing. Addiction is a consequence of learned experience and repetitions of patterns. Is alcoholism in the genes? The answer is no. In the science of epigenetics, it's been found that it's the perception of your environment that controls genes. You're not a victim of your genes because you're the one who can change your environment-or, more importantly, change your perception of your environment- and thus change your response to it".

Dr. Lipton suggests a Ted Talk, "Everything you think you know about addiction is wrong?" Article from Dr. Lipton's website blog dated July 28, 2015.

There are dozens of medical data on habits, compulsions, and addictions. Still, the bottom line is it all begins in the brain, fed through our thoughts and intentions, facilitated by the law of attraction, and it is from there where the rewiring process begins. Below are some simple steps you can take to break any habit, compulsion, or addiction.

For full disclosure, I am not a doctor or a Clinical Psychologist; my views on addictions are born from studying alternative methods and forming my own opinions on the subject. Please see a licensed professional to help overcome addictions; withdrawal from substance abuse can be life- threatening.

CHALLENGE: THE 7 METHOD

Acknowledge and face the problem. Begin by being 100% honest with yourself. Please write down the habits or addictions and what it has cost you. Does it cost you your health, job, family, or self-esteem? Read it out loud to yourself.

Identify the trigger points. Figure out what triggers this behavior. Identifying what causes you to return to the habit will clarify what needs to be done. If you smoke when you become anxious, finding the reasons and solutions for anxiety is an essential first step. Often the habit or addiction is a symptom of issues buried deep in the subconscious. (Steps to release subconscious blockage are discussed at a later date).

Replace. Expecting to cut out bad habits without replacing them is a recipe for failure. There was a reason you began the habit in the first place, and particular needs still have to be met. Replace bad habits with beneficial ones; don't just trade them for another bad one. Prepare the replacement in advance and eliminate the triggers if possible.

Forgive yourself. Give yourself a break. There is no sense in rehashing the could have, would have, or should have. It is counterproductive to live in the past no matter how many failed attempts—Pat yourself on the back for taking the right steps in moving forward and keep going.

Rewire your mind. Be consistent and persistent. Building new neural pathways with healthy habits takes time. Make a plan that includes meditation and visualization techniques. Listen to affirmations as you fall to sleep at night. Begin your morning by writing in your appreciation journal, and make clear intentions for the day.

Start small and slowly increase momentum. Take the easiest habit you wish to change first. Success attracts success, making it easier for more stubborn habits and addictions to fold.

Ask for help. Do not be ashamed or afraid to ask for help. An accountability partner is beneficial. Find someone you trust who is not afraid to tell you what you need to hear. Seek the assistance of a licensed professional.

ADDICTION CHANGES YOU, RECOVERY FORTIFIES YOU

makes you wiser and strong. you will love deeper and work smarter. You will smile more and find joy in the little things.

YOU NOT ONLY SURVIVE; YOU THRIVE.

Prepare four columns. In the first column, write down a list of habits or addictions you want to change. On the second column, write down what that habit or addiction is or has cost you.

On the third column, write down what you think triggers the behavior, and on the fourth column, write down the replacement (solution).

EXAMPLE:

Habit/addiction	the cost	the triggers	the replacement
I bite my nails	Painful, ugly, and embarrassing	Stress, especially when I'm going to give a presentation at work.	Learn some stress-releasing breathing techniques and positive affirmations.
I smoke one pack of cigarettes a day	Costly, my clothes smell like cigarettes, and my teeth are yellow.	Stress, the habit of smoking after meals.	Chew gum, go for a walk, see a doctor

REMEMBER: Be incredibly honest with yourself. It will help if you have self- awareness and an attitude for change.

MAKE PEACE WITH THE PAST

DAY-13

RELEASING THE WEIGHTS

Are you being weighed down by past hurts, fear, or trauma? Are you holding onto things you would rather forget?

What have you have been carrying around that is slowing you down or prohibiting you from moving forward?

Releasing the weights is crucial if you are to embrace the future.

People who have decided to forgive others for past hurts have healed physically and emotionally. John Hopkins Psychiatrist Dr. Karen Swartz says that forgiveness is good for our health and that holding grudges takes its toll.

When someone is stuck in an angry state, their body is also stuck in the form of adrenaline, in which there are negative health consequences such as high blood pressure, anxiety, depression, and a low immune system.

We can't erase the past, but bitterly holding grudges, seeking revenge, and blaming others only leave you depleted. Your life becomes one of mistrust, anxiety, and paranoia. Your relationships are affected negatively, and you sacrifice your health and sanity.

Some things are easier to forgive and move past, but others are too horrible to do the same. But there's a difference between seeing things as forgivable and having them be the consuming factor in your life. Forgiveness does not mean condoning; it's about not keeping the past alive by discussing, writing, envisioning, joining groups about, or spending years in therapy rehashing it.

The basis of cognitive-behavioral therapy, which has been scientifically proven to be very effective, is that your thoughts drive your feelings and emotions and, in turn, drive your behavior. Some historical information is needed, but the focus is primarily on developing more effective ways of coping with life (moving forward).

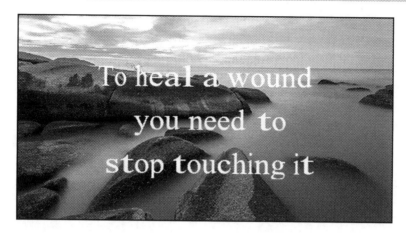

To heal a wound
you need to
stop touching it

Negative experiences gave you contrast and have made your preferences clear; now, it's time to focus on those preferences, forgive others; especially yourself and release the weights.

This following process is very useful in helping you release any residual anchors that are weighing you down.

Acknowledge - Accept - Appreciate - Advance

ACKNOWLEDGE
Acknowledge your anger and resentment. Take the time to let it out, vent, and release. Cry, scream, hit your pillow, box, etc. Let out your emotions in one session if possible but, do not dwell on them after the initial release.

ACCEPT
Accept your part in it, _if_ any, and forgive yourself.

APPRECIATE
Show appreciation for the possible lessons you've learned.

ADVANCE
Move on. Leave the negative past behind. There is a big difference between superficially bringing up the past and deep-diving into where feelings and emotions lie. Unless your experience can help others and you can recall without feeling weighed down, you may be doing more harm than good by going there.

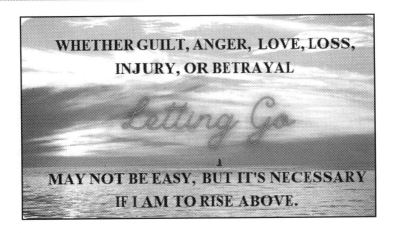

WHETHER GUILT, ANGER, LOVE, LOSS,
INJURY, OR BETRAYAL

Letting Go

MAY NOT BE EASY, BUT IT'S NECESSARY
IF I AM TO RISE ABOVE.

WRITE YOUR OWN STORY

Everyone has a story; who you are, what you do, where you've been, where you're going. But if your story doesn't please you or you wish it were different in some aspects, you need to TELL a different story.

Your new story may not change the past, but it will create the future, so tell the story you wish to live and be proud to share.

The stories you choose to tell impact whether or not you move forward in the desired direction. If you wish for a better life, tell a better life story.

Rewriting your story does not mean lying; it means picking out the aspects of your life you appreciate, are proud of, and wish more of.

It is talking about what you want and what you're striving for. It's looking at your life with optimism and excitement. It's sharing your story in a motivating and inspiring fashion.

No one can write your story; only you have that power.

CHALLENGE:

Clearing the Past Appreciation Letter:

- Write a list of names of people you feel hurt, disappointed, or let you down.

- Write a letter to a person or persons on your list: Include; <u>Acknowledge</u>, <u>Accept</u>, and <u>Appreciate</u> elements in your letters; destroy the letters when finished.

You may find this exercise difficult and emotional, but do not give up. The appreciation letter method is powerful because your focus is on forgiveness and moving on. Continuously reliving negative past experiences will not help you heal; it will only bring negative feelings to the surface and make those experiences current.

Remember, choosing to move on through forgiveness and positive focus does not mean condoning terrible behavior. It does not mean that what has happened is right and void of punishment. It means caring about yourself so much that you are willing to drop the anchor and make peace with the past.

Past suffering is an opportunity to learn valuable lessons and to develop a strong, resilient, positive character that will only propel you forward with confidence.

BONUS CHALLENGE

In a paragraph or two, write your story the way you wish it to be. (write in present tense)

ACKNOWLEDGE YOUR WINS

DAY-14

THE PHYSIOLOGICAL AND PSYCHOLOGICAL

Have you ever wondered why most people tend to have distinct memories of negative occurrences? Why do we vividly remember the terrible fall, the horrible scene, the embarrassing situation, or a conversation gone bad?

Recalling negative memories, experiences, and mistakes more than successes is typical, and understanding the reason is essential to direct our thoughts in a more positive direction.

Professor Nass, who co-authored "The Man Who Lied to His Laptop: What Machines Teach Us About Human Relationships," writes, "The brain handles positive and negative information in different hemispheres,"

Negative circumstances generally produce intense emotions that require more thinking and focus. We tend to ruminate, obsess and replay negative situations in our heads, and share this information with others, reinforcing that thought in our brains.

Low Self-Esteem

is like driving through life with your hand brake on.

Maxwell Maltz-

EARLY PROGRAMMING

Another reason most tend to focus on negativity may be due to information received as children. Do you remember being lectured more than being praised? Did it seem your parents or teachers pointed out your flaws and overlooked your accomplishments?

Did you grow up in a household where physical punishment was normal? Do you remember the lectures, scolding, warnings, and punishments vividly, and do they bring up certain emotions even now? Are you beginning to understand the power of words, actions, and emotions? No wonder we grow up obsessing over what we did wrong instead of what we did right! Why you may feel you'll never be good enough, feel shame, embarrassment, fear of backlash, and hold back from pursuing your dreams.

These adverse, traumatic events bring out deep emotions that the brain quickly remembers. It is no wonder that negative thinking comes easy for many.

Be aware of another adverse effect of negative childhood programming that is likely to be passed down. The reason you do or say certain things is because that's what you're used to.

Knowing that you have a choice can change the cycle and ensure that you pass along positive, productive skills to new generations.

BE YOUR ADVOCATE

Stop underestimating yourself. Stop picking yourself apart. Stop focusing on your perceived flaws. Stop being your biggest and harshest critic. It is good to acknowledge your role in lousy behavior but do not get stuck there. Take responsibility, pivot to the solution, and move on.

Be your advocate, recall good memories, talk about your accomplishments; brag about yourself (in specific settings, of course.) Appreciate your unique qualities and abilities. Think about your achievements and wins.

Please do not shy away from compliments, and stop talking others out of giving them to you. You are worthy of praise, especially from yourself. People who have been conditioned not to feel good enough are uncomfortable with this type of attention. Are you?

Be confident. Too many days are
wasted comparing ourselves to others and wishing to be
someone we're not. Everyone has their strength.

Accept yourself and be proud of who you are.
Many issues can be avoided if we first learn to
respect, honor, and love ourselves.

THE POKER CHIP THEORY

It is essential to accept yourself and all your successes, past and current. This acknowledgment has a massive impact on your self-esteem, and your self- esteem has a significant effect on your quality of life. Self-esteem is like poker chips.

Successful people confidently walk around with a pile of poker chips, while less confident people may have only a few. If a person with a low amount of chips plays against someone with a big pile of chips, guess who will win? The more chips you have, the more risks you are willing to take. How many chips do you have?

When you purposely think about your past successes, the "Law of Attraction" gives you another thought to match the prior one. Soon, you begin to think of more success and feel good and confident, which spurs more future success.

One positive thought = one poker chip.

Confidence is a state of mind and can be improved by practicing positive self-talk. Learn to treat yourself with respect, walk tall, and say kind words to yourself. You set the standard for how others see you and ultimately treat you.

CHALLENGE:

Success Inventory

Write a list of your successes and what you do well, no matter how insignificant you may still feel it is.

Example:

1. I was the lead in a school play.
2. I had a pretty successful lemonade stand in the summer when I was ten.
3. I am the best in my family at checkers.
4. I can take an engine apart and put it back together.

DAY-15

RECALL YOUR SUCCESSES

Many factors such as age, opportunities, geography, and social economics may determine how many and the level of your accomplishments up to this point, but remember that success is relevant and very personal.

Your future holds endless success stories that you will later recall and feel proud of and appreciate.

ACCOMPLISHMENT LOG

Keep a log of your successes. Display your certificates, awards, newspaper clippings, photos, etc., as a reminder of what you have accomplished. Recall the list of what you want to be, do, or have, and add them to your success list as you achieve them.

Research shows that surrounding yourself with testimonial items of your successes psychologically impacts your mood, attitude, and behavior.

Start getting comfortable with displaying your accomplishments. Hang the photo of the fish you caught.

Proudly display the trophy you won at the county fair when you were ten. Frame your shark tooth collection.

You have total control over your environment, so proudly display your success symbols, big or small, which will significantly boost your self-esteem.

CHALLENGE:

- Put together your accomplishment log in whichever form you like. The key is to refer to it often and add to it as time goes on.

- If you are a parent or a teacher, be sure to encourage your children or students to put together their own accomplishment log and display.

Do this exercise daily for a minimum of three weeks; soon, it will become an easy habit and may be scaled down.

You and only you are responsible for how you feel. Happiness is an inside job, and it begins with self-care, self-acknowledgment, and self-love.

Remember

YOU HAVE BEEN CRITICIZING YOURSELF
FOR YEARS, AND IT HASN'T WORKED.

TRY APPROVING OF YOURSELF
AND SEE WHAT HAPPENS.

LOUISE HAY-

BONUS CHALLENGE: THE MIRROR

The mirror exercise is based on the principle that we all need acknowledgment from ourselves.

Before bedtime, stand in front of a mirror and look directly into your eyes for a few seconds. Then begin giving yourself kudos for the success of the day. Talking to yourself may feel a little strange at first, but no one ever has to know. Make sure you maintain eye contact throughout the exercise and say, "I love you" to yourself at the end. Then take another few seconds to look deep into your eyes one more time. It is essential not to criticize yourself.

This exercise is not silly nor stupid; it is powerful. You are developing a relationship with YOU, learning to trust and rely on your higher self.

It is not anyone else's job to love, take care of, or make you happy. That responsibility rests on you, and this exercise can have a massive impact on your level of self-care.

EXAMPLE:

Look in the mirror for a few seconds. Then say something like: (say your name) *I appreciate you for deciding to take the thirty-one-day challenge. I love that you're developing good habits so that you will get more done. I appreciate that you took your time writing in your journal this morning.*

Thank you for having the courage to initiate the conversation today. I'm proud that you chose a healthy lunch and that you went out for an afternoon walk.

I love that you made time to read and relax. You got this! I love you.

EXAMINE YOUR BELIEFS

DAY-16

A BELIEF IS ONLY A THOUGHT THAT YOU KEEP THINKING

You will most likely manifest adverse limiting circumstances if you have negative, limiting beliefs. In turn, if you have positive, empowering beliefs, you will manifest wanted events. The key is to evaluate and challenge your current belief system, recognize any limiting belief, and make a conscious effort to change it.

If you believe you are worthless, it does not mean you are; it means you choose to see yourself worthless. If you think you're not smart enough, you decide to believe you are not smart enough. If you believe you do not deserve prosperity or happiness, it is because you believe you do not deserve it, not because it's true.

Limiting beliefs are detrimental to your well-being and can hold you back from ever achieving the life you want. Your subconscious mind will pick up negativity, worry, fear, and limiting suggestions. It will accept them as true and will work to make them true through manifestation.

Many people will argue that they experience negativity first and then feel bad about it. They say, "I'm fat because I see that I'm fat when I look in the mirror."

This is one of those "what came first" mind twisters, but the reality is that if you see yourself as fat, the mind starts to believe it and has to create the manifestation to match that thought, not the other way around.

Changing body image beliefs is especially challenging because the image or physical pain is a constant reminder of "what is," and every time we focus on the "what is," the "what is" continues to prove itself right.

There are two different approaches you could take.

- Practice the thought of what <u>can be</u> while pretending it already is. Pretend; act like it is different than what it is. You must imagine, visualize, and believe that it is different before it can be different.

- Only focus on the things that are pleasing, uplifting, and that bring you joy.

You do not need to convince yourself that you've reached the perfect weight; you have to stop focusing on the fact that you have not reached that goal yet.

Instead, look for things you can appreciate about yourself now and focus there. That focus will raise your overall vibration, and you will be in the receiving mode, ready for the universe to guide you to the ideas and circumstances that will help you reach those goals.

THE LANGUAGE OF CREATION

Notice if when you have negative thoughts, you verbally express them in the negative present tense, such as. "I'm so stupid." "I'll never amount to anything." "I hate myself for what I did." "I'll probably forget." "I'm going to be late." "I don't like this or that." Those are negatively charged present tense statements, most likely with a strong belief and emotion attached.

Begin the practice of using the same logic for positive thoughts.

don't say...	instead say...
I want to be...	I am...
I'm going to be...	I do...
I wish I were...	I have...
If only...	My experience is...
Why do I have to be...	I like...
Someday I will...	I love that...
I will be happy when...	I am happy about...

Whether or not you have had years of negative and limiting beliefs, what's important is that you understand that you have a choice and can change this now.

You can choose to take personal responsibility and guide your thoughts toward how you want things. Your thoughts have power, but you have power over your thoughts.

It may help you know that brain research indicates that with enough positive self-talk positive visualization combined with training, coaching, and practice, anyone can learn to do almost anything, including changing one's life and body.

CHALLENGE:

Please write down your current beliefs about the subjects below, then REPLACE them with positive phrases.

What is your belief about money and success? Example: "Money is hard to make."

Change the belief, Example: "It's easy to make money; others are doing it, so can I."

What is your belief about relationships? Example: "Everyone cheats on their partner."

Change the belief, Example: "There are many healthy relationships based on trust."

What are your beliefs about your health, body, and looks? Example: "I'm always tired." "I'm ugly." "I hate my hair."

Change the belief, Example: "I have plenty of energy when I do what I like." "I'm beautiful." "I love my gorgeous curls; women pay hundreds for what I was born with."

What are your beliefs about your job/career? Example: "I always get passed up for promotions."

Change the belief: "My work is valued, and I'm moving up at a perfect pace."

Shattering limiting beliefs

takes time, repetition, and consistency. You may not

believe everything you say right away, but practice positive

self-speak every day, and soon you will notice positive

changes.

DREAM AND ENVISION

DAY-17

I hope that you have allowed yourself to think about everything you want to have or experience by this point. Do not worry if you are not yet crystal clear because by writing a list of things you want to be, do, or have, you have already begun the first part of the envisioning process.

By believing that anything is possible and believing in yourself, you put yourself in a state of ALLOWING, ready, and open for all of your desires to come flooding in.

DAYDREAMING

A large-scale Harvard University study found that our minds wander 47% of the time. Another study found that 96% of adults daydream at least once a day.

Daydreaming helps you develop problem-solving strategies, according to Dr. Trivedi, Professor of psychiatry at UT Southwestern Medical Center.

David B. Feldman, department of counseling psychology at Santa Clara University, found that structured daydreaming coupled with imagination is not only motivating but can help you navigate through possible obstacles.

Research published in 2009 in the Journal Proceedings of the National Academy of Sciences suggested that the brain areas that allow people to solve complex problems become more active during daydreaming and may distract our attention from immediate tasks to solve other, more important ones.

Many people have come up with essential inventions and breakthroughs while daydreaming. There is enough research to suggest that focused daydreaming is beneficial and will help inspire you to reach your goals.

Are your daydreams structured? Do you use your imagination to envision those dreams? Have you ever had dreams about making a living doing what you enjoy doing? It is possible, and many people are making a living out of doing what they love.

Professional athletes and video gamers get paid for playing games. Comedians get paid for making people laugh etc. Can you think of other examples?

Balance daydreaming with living in the present. It would help if you experienced both to intentionally create the life you wish to live.

VISION

A vision is a detailed description, a mental picture complete with color, sounds, smells, tastes, feelings, and emotions. The act of envisioning is powerful because the mind can not distinguish between fantasy and reality.

When you visualize your goals as already complete, it creates a conflict (structural tension) in your subconscious mind between what you're envisioning and what you are currently living.

> **I visualize to the point that I know exactly what I want to do; dive, glide, stroke, flip, reach the wall, hit the split time to the hundredth, then swim back again for as many times I need to finish the race.**
> Michael Phelps-

Your subconscious mind works to resolve that conflict by turning your current reality into the new one. The "Law of Attraction" begins to gather all the components necessary to make that thought a reality, but remember, it does not happen instantaneously, so you must practice visualizing it first.

Once you begin to visualize correctly, you will notice that you wake up in the morning with new ideas. Some of the best ideas will be in the shower, driving to work, taking a walk, and right after meditation.

Notice new motivation levels, sharp instincts, gut feelings, and intuition. You begin to move out of your comfort zone, become more curious, and ask questions.

Listen to your guidance system. If it feels good, you are on the right path; if it does not, pause, evaluate, and adjust.

PROPER VISUALIZATION

The key to effective visualization is to visualize in the present tense. If you see your dreams in the future, then in the future, they will stay.

Do not dream about the car you will have; visualize the vehicle you <u>do</u> have. Pretend your dreams have already come true. What color, make, and model is the car? How does it handle, what does it smell like?

VISUALIZATION

**IS THE HUMAN BEING'S
VEHICLE TO THE FUTURE,
GOOD, BAD, OR IN DIFFERENT.
IT'S STRICTLY IN YOUR CONTROL.**

Earl Nightingale-

Conjuring intense emotion is a critical step in this process. How do you feel in the drivers' seat and with your hands on the steering wheel? This visualizing and dreaming technique is the difference between obtaining all of your desires or your desires being just beyond reach.

7 AREAS OF SUCCESS FOR A BALANCED LIFE

Make sure your visualization process includes these seven areas of your life:

1. Work/Career
2. Finances
3. Recreation/Free time
4. Health and Fitness
5. Relationships
6. Personal Goals
7. Community Contribution

At this stage of the journey, you do not have to worry about HOW you're going to achieve your goals. Worrying about what actions to take will only slow you down. Worrying and anxiety are negative emotions. Believe first; the "how" will follow.

CHALLENGE:

Write down what you would like to create or experience in each category.

1. Work/Career
2. Finances
3. Recreation/Free time
4. Health and Fitness
5. Relationships
6. Personal Goals
7. Community Contribution

Once you have your answers written down, it is time to visualize. Sit or lie down, close your eyes, and begin to imagine what you have described in the exercise. Be as descriptive as possible. How does it look, feel, and smell? What are the textures and colors? Are there sounds? Does it feel fun? Do you feel happy, excited, comfortable, satisfied?

It is essential to envision your desires as if it is happening in the current time. Do not see yourself doing or having these things as though you are watching yourself in a movie. If your vision is in the future, you will never reach it. You MUST envision it as if it is happening now. If you do this correctly, you will experience deep emotion.

EXAMPLE:

- What are your ideal income and monthly cash flow? How much do you have in the bank?

- What does your home look like, where is it located? What kind of landscaping do you see?

- What kind of car do you drive, what color is it? Does it smell new?

- What do you do for a living, whom do you work with? Where is your office or shop located?

- What are you doing for fun, what are your hobbies, where do you go on vacation?

- What is your ideal body? You are healthy, strong, and in shape. How does it feel to enjoy healthy, great-tasting food and drink plenty of water? You are relaxed, happy, and joyful. You are energetic, enthusiastic, and excited.

- Do you have children? How many? What kind of person is your mate, and what type of relationship do you two enjoy?

- Are you back in school, taking classes, learning a new language?

- What charities do you donate to, how do you volunteer your time? How do you help the community?

Do not rush this process. Take your time and prepare for it. Reserve a quiet spot with minimal distractions. Silence your cell phone and give your undivided attention to the pictures, sounds, and smells in your head.

Envision as much as you have time. Pick one or two subjects to envision daily and witness how quickly your dreams come true.

GROW IN SELF-CONFIDENCE

DAY-18

IT'S ALL ABOUT THE ATTITUDE

"I know I can do anything I put my mind to. I am confident in my abilities, talents, skills, and inner strength to create all that I desire. I like myself. I'm good-looking, I'm smart, I can be creative and fun to be with. I'm quite amazing".

Me-

How did it feel while reading the above paragraph? Some people have a problem complimenting themselves. Have you heard comments such as, "don't be a show-off, showboat, braggart, selfish, self-centered"?

Our society has created enormous insecurities and feelings of guilt and shame for being proud of ourselves.

CONFIDENCE OR ARROGANCE?

There is a thin line between confidence and arrogance. Sometimes it is appropriate to self- promote, such as on a job interview, on a date, or meeting new people.

People like and are attracted to others with self-confidence. They seem at ease and sure of themselves, and this promotes trust. Confidence is contagious, and you may inspire others to boost theirs.

Beware that your bragging isn't to make someone else look bad to cover up your insecurities; it sends out a negative vibe.

WHAT IS SELF-CONFIDENCE?

Self-Confidence is caring, loving, and honoring yourself. Self-confidence is when you know your self-worth and trust your judgment and abilities. It is accepting and loving yourself no matter what others think.

A confident person does not look to others for acceptance and reassurance; they look inward.

It is doing what you believe is right, even if others don't agree with you.

It is going the extra mile, challenging yourself, taking risks, and thinking outside the box. It is seeing and admitting your mistakes and self adjust. It is accepting praise and compliments from others graciously.

BUILDING YOURSELF UP.

Successful people with confidence make self-care a priority.

You must be your advocate and promoter. Do not rely on anyone else to build you up; self-confidence is an inside job!

If you rely on someone outside yourself to build you up, you will set yourself up for disappointment instead.

> HOW CAN ANYONE SEE HOW GREAT YOU ARE IF YOU CAN'T SEE IT YOURSELF?

Take compliments and stop self-deprecating comebacks.

If someone says you look nice, say thank you, and that's it! Stop following up compliments with, "Oh, really, I hate how I look."

BRAG TO YOURSELF

Begin to build your self-confidence by self- bragging. Tell yourself about how smart you are, how funny you are, how confident you are, how courageous you are etc.

You want to visualize and "act as if." Congratulate yourself for accepting this challenge and getting this far—Pat yourself on the back every day. Once you make it a habit of following this method of self-congratulation, the manifestation will eventually follow.

TAKE CARE OF YOURSELF AND YOUR SURROUNDINGS

Take care of your physical needs. Eat healthy food, drink more water, move more. The outside reflects what you put inside.

Have a consistent hygiene routine. Take care to be clean, and smell fresh. Keep an organized and clean living space; messes and clutter create stress and rob you of time.

BE ASSERTIVE

Self-confidence is also about being assertive and setting boundaries. Live on your terms, and do not allow anyone to hold you back.

Remember, people will only do as much as you enable them to do. Reach deep for your superpower. Ask for feedback.

ENGAGE IN ACTIVITIES AND HOBBIES THAT BRING YOU JOY

Do what you love, play more, take adventures, teach, mentor, and support others. Continue to learn.

Gain knowledge through reading and be curious about the world around you. Go beyond your comfort zone and try new things. Be productive and well-rounded.

YOU CANNOT BENEFIT THOSE YOU LOVE IF YOU DON'T LOOK AFTER YOURSELF FIRST!

Write an appreciation letter to yourself. Be as detailed and expressive as possible. This exercise is incredibly powerful. It will help you shed old habits of insecurity and low self-esteem.

You know the difference between arrogance and confidence. Practice loving, caring, supporting, and believing in yourself.

Don't hold back. Make this a heartfelt, personal love letter to yourself. This may be challenging at first but give yourself a few sentences; after that, you'll be off to the races.

Begin your letter with:

Dear; (your name),

I love you so much because...

UNBLOCK

DAY-19

TIME TO EVALUATE

This is a good point in the challenge to evaluate your progress and ask some crucial questions about yourself.

Have I been consistent and determined to stay on schedule? Have I read all the material, completed the exercises, and applied what I have learned?

If so, congratulations! Sticking to something and creating new habits can be challenging, considering everything we deal with daily.

But despite your best efforts, are there areas in your life that remain unsatisfying? Are you running on willpower, and are you starting to feel fatigued? Are you holding on to a set of beliefs that keep you stuck in one or more areas of your life?

THE PATTERN-SEEKING BRAIN

Consider that our thought patterns result from experience, upbringing, and daily interactions. No two people are alike, so we each carry different thought vibrations for specific areas of our lives.

You may have a positive career thought pattern, and so you are successful in your career.

Some people grew up with parents that loved and respected each other, and so their beliefs of a loving partnership are positive, so they enjoy successful relationships.

Others may have grown up in a financially stable environment, so money isn't an issue.

The mind loves patterns and consistency, so the only way to change negative thought patterns is to build new ones subconsciously.

Your subconscious is like a computer hard drive that processes 4 billion bits of information per second—a place where memories are stored and where habits are formed. *Dr. Bruce H. Lipton, Ph.D.*

If you are experiencing a blockage in one or all areas of your life, it isn't because your subconscious sabotages you; you have outdated programs requiring deleting and replacing.

WHOLE-BRAIN INTEGRATION

"Brain Dominance theory" is another crucial factor to consider when deleting and replacing deep-rooted subconscious beliefs.

Brain Dominance research findings indicate that each hemisphere specializes in different functions, processes other information, and deals with various problems. The goal is to "cross-talk" the two hemispheres and achieves a whole-brain state to change subconscious beliefs. The Missing Piece In Your Life!" *Robert M. Williams, M.A.*

You will have a chance to try this technique in the challenge.

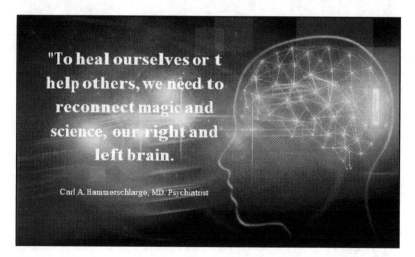

The following three-step process will help you effectively communicate with your subconscious and remove any blockages holding you back.

IDENTIFY IT

CLEAR IT

REPLACE IT

What areas of your life do you find the most challenging, and there continues to be inner conflict? Where are you noticing resistance? Is it work, relationships, self-esteem, addictions, etc.?

ABOUT FAMILY LIFE:

You grew up in a dysfunctional household believing that dysfunction is normal.

You believe that marriage and children are hard work. You feel that divorce and single parenting are not only possible but probable.

About your love life:

If your love life has not turned out the way you wish it would, perhaps you have been cheated on or abandoned. Consequently, your belief about dating and relationships is that there is no such thing as a good relationship; that true love doesn't exist.

ABOUT YOUR HEALTH AND SELF-ESTEEM:

You get down on yourself with negative self-talk. You constantly second-guess yourself; you lack confidence, enthusiasm, and energy. You don't feel you deserve happiness and feel guilty for past choices. You are disappointed with your looks and body.

Social media has you believe you're inadequate and lacking.

Certain diseases run in your family, so you feel you will likely develop them.

About money:

You believe that the rich are greedy and that there is not enough for everyone. You think that you probably won't be rich because you were not born rich.

You hold onto things thinking there will not be more.

ABOUT JOB/CAREER

You are stuck doing a job you don't enjoy, and you settle because you feel you don't have a choice.

You feel taken for granted, disrespected, and under-compensated but are too scared to speak up? You feel you may not be good enough to deserve a raise or promotion.

ABOUT FRIENDSHIPS

Bullied in school, you grew up mistrusting and on alert. You were a victim of gossip or slander, so you believe all people are fake and will easily stab you in the back.

You believe that being alone and at arm's length from others is your best option.

You believe no one understands you or cares.

Do any of these scenarios resonate with you? Remember, the law of attraction matches you up with the vibration you carry about any subject, so you will most likely continue to make a beeline toward that type of person or circumstance unless you clear (delete and replace) that pattern of thought.

If you want to have more money, you must clear your negative beliefs about money. If you wish for better health and a physical image, you must remove the blockages that keep you from getting there. If you want healthy relationships, you must clear and replace those too.

CHALLENGE:

CLEAR IT

Now that you've identified the blockage, it is time to clear it with this quick and easy meditative process.

Make sure you are alone and free from distractions for at least 10 minutes. (turn off your electronic devices) Read through the exercise a few times to know what to do without stopping to reread it.

- Think of one limiting belief that you identified and wish to clear. You must focus on one belief at a time. For example, I haven't been able to find a perfect partner.

- Sit on a chair with your feet crossed at the ankles and your hands intertwined. Close your eyes and relax, but do not slouch.

- Take three deep breaths.

- Imagine a bright yellow light coming from the heavens slowly washing over you, starting from the top of your head to your feet and then expanding from your sides outward, further and further out. See yourself being surrounded by a big ball of sunshine.

- This ball of light that surrounds you gets bigger and bigger so that it's bigger than the room you are sitting in, and it continues to expand until it reaches the heavens and all around. This light is your inner being, source- energy, guide, god, angels, or universe. Feel the energy surrounding you, being you.

- While this light surrounds you, speak the blockage out loud.

EXAMPLE:

IDENTIFY IT "All men are liars and cheats, and I will never find a partner."

REPLACE the negative belief with a positive one. Thinking about and saying what you don't want continuously will only keep it present. Remember, the universe does not understand NO.

You must replace the thought with what you do want. This step is critical and will mean the difference between failure and success. You are rewiring, rebuilding, reprocessing.

EXAMPLE: "There are good men out there, and I am worthy of finding the man of my dreams." "I know many couples that have loving relationships." "I am deserving of true love," etc.

Continue to talk yourself into the new belief. After a few minutes, you should feel relief, but do not worry if you still feel some resistance; sometimes, it takes several rounds. Do this process for every limiting belief still active in your vibration.

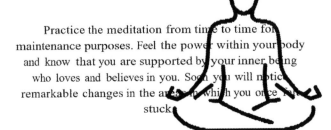

Practice the meditation from time to time for maintenance purposes. Feel the power within your body and know that you are supported by your inner being who loves and believes in you. Soon you will notice remarkable changes in the areas in which you once felt stuck.

YES, I CAN!

DAY-20

YOU EITHER CAN, CAN'T, OR WILL NOT.

How many times a day do you say "I can't"? How many times a day do you hear others say, "I can't?"

Today, some things are not humanly possible; for example, we cannot currently live to be 200 years old. Someday maybe, but most people use the word can't so casually that it is no longer heard as a negative, although it is. It is disempowering to believe we cannot do something.

The word (can't) implies that you have no way of doing, accomplishing, or finishing something in particular. It is a case-closed comment.

In essence, when you say I can't, you are saying that you would, but you either believe you cannot or you just will not.

Either way, saying "I can't" because you are trying to get out of something or do not believe in yourself is self-sabotage. If you don't want to do something, say you do not want to. The difference between not wanting to do something and cannot do something is about having a choice.

You may see this as just semantics, but words do matter.

"Whether you think you can, or you
think you can't, you're right."

Henry Ford-

Believing in yourself is necessary to move forward and plan your journey to what you want. If you lack confidence in your abilities and question your courage, in essence, you have stopped before getting very far.

Many people say, "I can't," when they mean, "I won't." They are either being disingenuous, fearing disapproval, or disappointing someone. If you do not wish to do something, it is okay to say, "no, I will not." Be honest with yourself and others. Trust your inner guidance and decision-making capabilities.

REMAIN VIGILANT

There will be times when self-doubt will slowly creep in. Remind yourself that you must replace thoughts with new ones to change habits, limiting beliefs, and negative thought frames.

Transforming your life into the one you want is a daily process. Every day take stock of how you are using your mind powers. Watch out for negative words like I can't, and start saying, "I can." Begin feeling comfortable with "I won't" as long as it comes from a place of choice and power.

CHALLENGE:

Write down some instances in which you- self-sabotaged because you didn't believe in yourself and told yourself you could not do it.

EXAMPLE:

- I didn't try out for the part.
- I didn't turn in the resume.
- I didn't go on a date.
- I didn't move to a new city.
- I didn't take the challenge.

Take your time, think it through, and analyze your choices. Pay attention to what you could have accomplished had you said: "I CAN."

Now convince yourself why you CAN do it.

EXAMPLE: Negative self-speak "I did not enter the race because I did not think I had the stamina to finish."

Positive self-speak replacement "I know I can finish the race because I am strong, agile, and I have been training for this."

BONUS CHALLENGE:

Pay close attention to your choice of words throughout the day. Pay attention to any "but" and "I can't."

Write down how many times you hear it in yourself and others. Practice catching yourself but quickly pivot to more empowering words.

It's all a matter of forming new habits by first becoming aware and then doing something about it.

DAY-21

WHEN THINGS DO NOT ENTIRELY TURN OUT THE WAY YOU ENVISIONED

It may be disappointing, and you may even begin to doubt your powers of thought when what you had in mind does not turn out the way you thought it should. BUT, what appears to be a misfortune may be an unexpected benefit.

For example: getting laid off from work may force you to go into business for yourself or go back to school. A missed flight may be the difference between life and death. Taking the wrong turn may cause you to find a shortcut or avoid traffic or a car accident. Being dumped is the reason for a new and fantastic relationship.

There is a path of least resistance to lead you to everything you desire, so instead of becoming frustrated, angry, and disappointed, become curious and optimistic. Be open and trust your inner being to lead you to what you want even if you do not quite understand it at the time; the unexpected path may pleasantly surprise you.

CHALLENGES AND OPPORTUNITIES

Learn to look at obstacles and negatives as opportunities. Opportunities to change and grow. How can you know what you want unless you first experience what you do not want?

Without negatives, we could not possibly experience nor appreciate the positive. Our most significant and profound dreams and wishes are born out of severe life negatives.

The person in a job they hate will wish (vibrationally ask) for a better job. The person in a toxic relationship will dream (vibrationally ask) for a good, loving relationship. A person with an illness will pray (vibrationally ask) for wellness and health. When someone cuts you off in traffic, you prefer (vibrationally ask) for courteous people on the road.

ALLOW YOURSELF TO BE INSPIRED THROUGH THE PATH OF LEAST RESISTANCE

Obstacles and negatives are necessary for growth; when you experience a negative emotion, you automatically ask for a better, more positive one. There is no way around it; you are always in the state of asking.

LEARN TO PIVOT

Whenever you are confronted with a negative experience or circumstance, ask yourself, "How can this serve me?" "What can I learn from this?" "What do I prefer?" "How can I change this?" Pivoting is an important skill to learn when taking control of any situation.

Do not get hung up on the "why did this happen?" Spend a minimal amount of time figuring out how this situation made itself into your experience. Once you have identified what you could have done differently, stop, and move on. If you overthink it and talk about it, you only keep it active.

Pivoting takes practice, so be patient. Before long, pivoting will become a healthy and empowering habit.

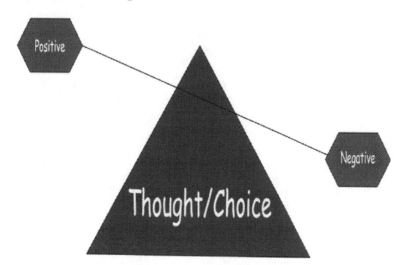

CHALLENGE:

Write about negative situations that turned out to have positive outcomes.

What are some challenges you have encountered that could have been opportunities?

EXAMPLE:

- I took the wrong turn, but I missed a bad accident.

- The pandemic is an opportunity to create ways to better connect with others. Video chatting has allowed me to see my grandchildren more often.

Blessings

MAYBE THE RESULT OF PERCEIVED
PROBLEMS, IT'S ALL IN THE PERSPECTIVE

DAY-22

ACKNOWLEDGE YOUR FEELINGS

At some point in our lives, we all experience incredibly overwhelming circumstances, such as a job loss, a breakup, a relapse, a death, etc. It is important to own that feeling while at the same time realizing that it will pass.

Trying to force happiness in the middle of a negative feeling is like stopping a runaway train. Instead, allow the emotion, let it speak, and remind yourself that your future does not need to be defined by such experiences.

Give yourself time to grieve. Loosen up the valve and release emotions; holding it in will only cause more physiological and physical pain.

Cry in the shower, hit a pillow, or drown out a nice scream with music. Exercise or go for a run, whatever you need to do to let it out.

Avoid the temptation to share your downs on social media; you will most likely regret it.

When you put your business on public display, you open yourself up for unproductive comments, criticism, embarrassment, and further abuse.

Talk with a trusted friend, mate, or parent. The act of talking it out, to let it out, is helpful as long as you don't linger there; let it out, and move on.

WHEN THINGS ARE FALLING APART

THEY MAY BE FALLING INTO PLACE

Using negative behaviors to numb the pain is temporary, leaving you feeling worse in the long run; instead, practice self-care by engaging in self-compassionate acts.

Stop beating yourself up for having negative feelings and thoughts.

Experiencing all levels of emotions is natural and necessary. Vulnerability is not weakness; it is a sign of strength that will ultimately help you move through the pain and heal.

When momentum has a hold of your negative emotions, go with it, but practice bouncing back at soon as possible. Usually, meditation, a nap, or a good night's sleep is enough to start again.

PREPARE FOR A COMEBACK

The more you practice thinking and talking about what you do want and being in appreciation, the easier it will be to regroup and recoup from a low.

The more you talk about **WHAT IS WORKING,** the more evidence you will see of things you desire.

Remember, every heartbreak, all the disappointments, challenges, and obstacles are opportunities to identify your preferences and shoot out into the universe a powerful desire that, if you allow it, will manifest itself to you.

CHALLENGE:
Write down an example of a difficult situation. Think through how to handle it best, knowing what you now know about the "Law of Attraction."

EXAMPLE:

The situation:

A parent has a terminal illness.

"I will do all I can to make sure my parent is comfortable and find some joy." "I will think about the good times and remind them of how much they are loved."

DAY-23

THOUGHTS VIBRATE AT CERTAIN FREQUENCIES

Recall the Japanese scientist and his water crystal experiment? The water crystals' shape changed depending on the words it was exposed to. Negative words produced distorted, ugly crystals, and positive words produced beautiful, nicely formed crystals.

If our bodies are over 60% water, what are the words that we use daily produce? What kind of self-talk do you habitually engage in? We must remind ourselves that the thoughts we choose to think impact what we experience; this is worth repeating.

Negative thoughts equal low vibration frequencies, and positive thoughts equal high vibration frequencies. Your emotions provide you feedback on what frequency, low or high, your thoughts are producing. Your thoughts attract other similar thoughts, referred to as the point of attraction.

Your point of attraction fluctuates all day between low and high, depending on your thinking. Extended and consistent high-frequency thoughts equal positive experiences, and the opposite is true for low-frequency thoughts. Again; worth repeating.

"IF WE UNDERSTOOD THE

POWER OF OUR THOUGHTS

we would guard them more closely. if we understood the awesome power of our words, we would prefer silence to almost anything negative. In our thoughts and words, we create our weaknesses and our strengths."

Betty Eadie-

THINKING IN THE NOW

You have the option to think in the past tense, present tense, or future tense. Most people default to past or future tense, reminiscing about past events or figuring out their future.

Learn to be PRESENT
yesterday is gone, tomorrow is not here, your power is NOW

The problem and stress lie when the past is negative or traumatic, and the future is uncertain and scary.

Do you live in the past, or are you mainly thinking about future possibilities, which may or may not be beneficial? If memories bring you joy, then go for it. If you find satisfaction thinking about your future as if it were in the present (visualizing), then do more of it, BUT your power is in the NOW! The present matters; from this point, future manifestations are born.

Pay attention, examine, ponder and feel what is happening now. Observe your surrounding and your emotions.

Practice and enjoy the experience of NOW. Be present and acknowledge what is happening in real-time. The past is gone, and the future is not here, but you are always in the NOW.

Spend 10% in the past, 10% in the future, and 80% in the present.

THE MOST IMPORTANT 45 MINUTES OF YOUR DAY

Jack Canfield, Author of Chicken Soup for the Soul, says that whatever you choose to think during the last 45 minutes of the day dramatically influences your sleep and how your next day turns out.

Our subconscious replays and processes this last input up to six times more often than anything else we experience during the day. Have you ever had a nightmare after watching a scary movie? The brain is very suggestible and does not differentiate fantasy from reality, and it develops patterns of thoughts that turn into manifestations.

Prepare the 45 minutes just before going to sleep wisely. Intend to have a good night's rest and to wake up energized and refreshed. Take the time to acknowledge your successes and write down what you intend to accomplish the next day.

Visualize what you see yourself achieving and conjure up the feelings those accomplishments will produce. Fall asleep listening to guided meditations or soft, soothing sounds such as rain, breach waves, or relaxing music, whatever helps you relax.

CHALLENGE:

Write down the answers to the following questions.

1. What type of books have you read lately? Write down the titles. Did those books make you smarter, happier, or cynical and sad?
2. What type of movies have you been watching? What kind of feelings did those movies produce in you? Sadness, horror, anxiety, joy, laughter, and happiness?
3. What are you mostly watching on tv/social media? News commentaries, gossip, reality tv, documentaries? What type of feelings does that content bring out in you?
4. What type of music do you listen to? What is the message in the lyrics? Does it conjure sad or happy memories? Does it make you cry, or does it make you dance?
5. What type of conversations do you typically engage in? Complaints, gossip, confrontational, pessimistic or positive, uplifting, encouraging, motivating, understanding?
6. How do you speak to your partner, children, parents? Condescending, sarcastic, mean, or disrespectful? Or respectful, loving, kind, attentive?
7. How do you speak to yourself? Are you critical and judgmental, or are you gentle, forgiving, and loving?
8. Do you have a bedtime routine? What is the last thing you do before you go to bed? Is it watching videos, checking messages, social media, electronic games, reading, meditation, bath, prayer, soothing music, loving conversations with your partner?

Analyze your answers. Make a plan to change your routine for the next three days. Keep a log of your observations.

UNDERSTANDING AFFIRMATIONS

DAY-24

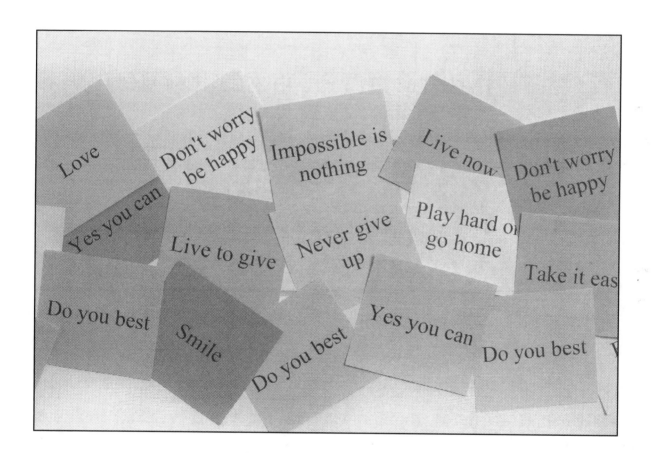

SELF-AFFIRMATIONS- SCIENTIFIC BACKED THEORY

Affirmations are brief phrases repeated frequently that encourage thoughts, attitudes, and behavior. MRI evidence suggests specific neural pathways are increased when we self-affirm. -Cascio et al., 2016.

Thought patterns turn into beliefs, and beliefs eventually turn into manifestations, so anything you repeat, you ultimately master by imprinting subliminal messages into your subconscious.

Corporations spend billions using affirmations to imprint their message or product into our minds, eventually loosening our wallets. Do food commercials make you hungry? Can you only eat one chip? Do you trust individual companies due to their familiarity factor? How many commercials come to mind? How about jingles or slogans? Affirmations are marketing genius because it works!

THE BENEFITS OF POSITIVE AFFIRMATIONS

Affirmations are mostly thought of as positive BUT beware; affirmations can also produce negative results.

Take a look at Some Essential Guidelines.

MAKE IT PERSONAL:
start with "I," or if it is in a group, start with "we."

MAKE IT PRESENT-TENSE:
such as "I am," "I love," or "I appreciate."

EXAMPLE:

- I am loved
- I appreciate my new bike
- We have a great relationship

WHEN YOU SAY NO, YOU ARE SAYING YES !

The Law of Attraction does not respond to words; it responds to the words' vibration, and you will know by the way you feel whether or not it is a positive high-frequency vibration or a low negative frequency vibration. Words matter because we have assigned meaning to them. Meanings conjure up specific feelings and indicate what you are about to create.

When you say, "I'm not going to eat junk food," the universe only hears "eat junk food." Most importantly, what are the feelings associated with "I'm not going to"? Deprivation perhaps?

When instead you say, "I'm going to eat healthy food," the omission of the word "not" feels much better, for "I'm going to eat healthy food" is getting something, not being deprived of it.

Another example is "I will get over my fear of losing that person." Can you spot the words that should be omitted for the sentence to be a positive affirmation?

If you said, "get over" and "fear," you're right. Getting over implies a problem you have to overcome, and although true, you are focusing on the issue by expressing it.

When you use the word fear, not only are you focusing on the issue, but the universe only hears "fear," so what do you think that word is going to attract? More fear! A better way to affirm when you wish to get over someone is, "I look forward to a new amazing relationship."

When crafting an affirmation, it's sometimes helpful to first write down the problem and then write down the solution.

Remember:

- Make it present tense: If said as if in the future, it will stay in the future.

- Be Brief: Memorize and repeat the affirmation throughout the day.

- Be Specific: Vague affirmations produce vague results.

- Include an action word: loving, expressing, winning, feeling, etc.

- Include at least one dynamic feeling word: enjoying, adoring, thrilled, excited, exhilarated, peacefully, astounding, etc.

- You can only affirm for yourself: You can not create for someone else or change someone else's behavior.

- It doesn't have to be true; yet: The universe does not differentiate fantasy from reality, so affirm what you want.

TIP

- Repeat your affirmations at least three times per day. The best times are when you wake up in the morning, in the middle of the day, and just before you fall asleep.

- Be consistent.

- Say them out loud when possible.

- Pair it with envisioning and feeling what you are affirming.

- Write your affirmations on post-it notes, index cards, or colorful pieces of paper; write them on the bathroom mirror with a marker.

- Say your affirmations at times, such as driving in the car, waiting in line, brushing your teeth, in the shower, etc.

- Listen to affirmations while falling asleep.

CHALLENGE:

Practice writing and saying affirmations.

Find clever ways of crafting, saying, and jotting down affirmations. Play with the process and find ways that work best for you.

Sample Affirmations:

- Everything always works out for me.

- I am loving life.

- I am proudly receiving my diploma.

- I am confidently speaking at the meeting.

- I am excited about skydiving.

- I love traveling by plane.

- I'm earning money easily and quickly.

- I love and appreciate myself.

THE EMOTIONAL SCALE

DAY-25

THOUGHTS VIBRATE AT CERTAIN FREQUENCIES

e·mo·tion
əˈmōSH(ə)n/
noun
plural noun: emotions

1. A natural instinctive state of mind deriving from one's circumstances, mood, or relationships with others.

Simply put, we are vibrational beings living in a vibrational, constantly expanding world and adding to its expansion through our thoughts.

The "Law of Attraction" manages the vibrational frequencies by matching one frequency to another like a magnet.

The Emotional Scale Chart below is an easy visual to help you understand the range of emotions so that you may be able to navigate the scale with ease. Knowing your point of attraction is beneficial to choosing a better feeling.

Make it a point to be at the top half of the scale spectrum at least 80% of the time. It is necessary to have some negative emotions to expand (grow, want more, create). Don't be hard on yourself for ending up at the bottom half of the scale; move up as soon as possible.

When you find yourself exhibiting feelings in the lower half of the scale, try to reach for thoughts that feel slightly better.

It is impossible to make huge jumps from one end of the scale to another, from grief to happiness. If you are in despair, try for anger, then when you are in anger, try for blame, then disappointment, then for hope. When you manage to hope, you are in the vicinity of the scale's positive region.

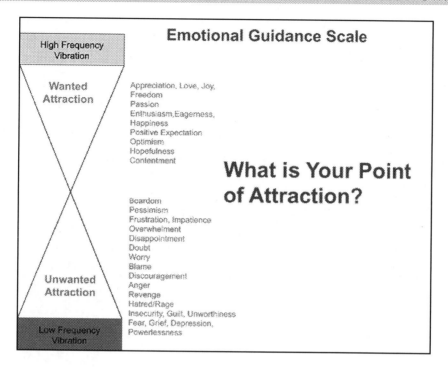

Because formed habits have deep roots, the key is to make it a daily practice to create new patterns by choosing the best thought.

You can choose to criticize or upbuild, love, or hate. You can focus on what you want rather than what you don't want. You can point at the negative about someone or choose to see them in a positive light.

You can decide to pick yourself apart or build yourself up. You can choose, you can choose, you can choose!

Learning to pivot from a negative thought to a positive one takes practice and will soon become a habit if you are consistent. Do not get obsessed with watching your every word; just quickly and gently choose what to focus on. The first step is awareness, for you cannot change what you do not acknowledge.

"WHEN YOU REACH FOR THE THOUGHT, THAT FEELS BETTER

the universe

is now responding differently to you because of that effort, and so, the things that follow you get better and better too.

SO IT GETS EASIER TO REACH FOR THE THOUGHT THAT FEELS BETTER BECAUSE YOU ARE ON EVER-INCREASING IMPROVING PLATFORMS THAT FEEL BETTER."

ABRAHAM HICKS-

CHALLENGE:

Spend the rest of the day acutely aware of your point of attraction. When you catch yourself thinking a negative thought write it down along with the corresponding feeling. If you cannot write, try to keep a mental note and write it down as soon as you can. When you have time, go back to your notes, write a positive to counteract the negative. Keep writing until your feelings change about that negative. Practice writing and saying affirmations.

EXAMPLE:

While at the drugstore, the clerk quickly and efficiently rings me up. I dig in my bag for my wallet, but I cannot find it. I think the people behind me and the clerk are getting impatient. I am embarrassed, and I immediately leave.

On my way to my car, I had a coarse conversation with myself. "How can I be so foolish...the wallet was on the kitchen counter. All those people were looking at me, judging me". I begin to feel angry and frustrated at myself and the other people in line, including the clerk.

If I have a pen and paper in my car, I sit for a few minutes and write down some positives to calm my anger. I have an inner dialogue if I do not have something to write with.

For Example, I was feeling:

- Down on myself for forgetting my wallet.
- Angry at the people in line and the clerk for being impatient.

Instead, I could say to myself:

- It is not the end of the world; I am getting better at remembering things. I will remember to ensure my wallet is in my purse before leaving the door. I have no control over what others think. Most people are understanding. I'm sure this has happened to them at some point.

It's all about choice. Choose productive thoughts, and you'll experience wanted results.

what someone else thinks about
me is none of my business

INSPIRED ACTION

DAY-26

INSPIRATION IS KEY

Many people take action in haste, ill-prepared, and out of fear or impatience. Some fear that if they do not act "now," they will lose an opportunity. Others take action because they believe that not being proactive is not being out of control and perhaps lazy. But, jumping into action without being in alignment is like jumping out of a plane without a parachute.

Look to your inner being to guide you by listening to your gut, intuition, feeling sure is different from fear-based action.

Ask yourself, "what is the motive of the action I am about to take?" "How does it feel?" "am I happy and satisfied with this decision?" "am I uncertain, insecure, going back and forth?".

Some will argue that success does not happen by sitting around and waiting for it to come to you, that you have to go out and get it! True but, if you are running around trying to make things happen without feeling ready or inspired, chances are you will be frustrated and going about it the long, hard way. There is an easier, joyful path to getting what you want, and that is through inspired action.

How Will I know?

When my actions are inspired, my steps are effortless

The way to operate from inspiration is knowing when you are feeling inspired. It is important to note that there are negative and positive inspirations.

If you are in a bad mood and in a negative feeling, most likely, whatever you are "inspired" to do is also negative and will probably lead to dire consequences. On the other hand, if you are inspired while feeling great, happy, and optimistic, the inspiration will lead you to positive desires.

The universe bends backward to give you what you want, continually laying at your feet opportunities and circumstances to propel you forward onto your life's desires, not once but over and over again; you have to be in the right frequency to spot it.

Prepare to spot the signs of inspiration. Positive inspiration is born out of being in alignment with your inner being, for it is from that high frequency that the universe matches you up with your desires.

The first and most important "Action" should be to continue to write appreciations in your journal daily, preferably first thing in the morning. Intend to have a good day, visualize, and say an affirmation.

FIND WAYS TO HAVE FUN, SEE THE BEST IN YOURSELF AND OTHERS, AND GIVE YOURSELF A BREAK. WHEN YOU ARE BUSY BEING HAPPY, LIFE- CHANGING OPPORTUNITIES AND CIRCUMSTANCES PRESENT THEMSELVES.

Don't get bogged down with the planning process, the analyzing, and overanalyzing. This may seem counterintuitive if you're still carrying old limiting beliefs of "no pain, no gain" or believe that working hard is the only way to get what you want.

> **WHEN**
>
> **IN**
>
> **DOUBT**
>
> trust
>
> your gut

ACTION is involved, but it is inspired by positive feelings and the next logical step. Do not postpone, drag on, push on, nor ignore the clear universal signs.

If you receive the signals and it feels right, go for it.
Make the call, go there, write the song, study this, say that, say yes, or say no. You are the creator, trust yourself and hone in on your instincts.

PROCRASTINATION

Procrastination is an indicator that you are not yet inspired to take action. It is essential to identify the areas you are habitually putting off and avoiding in your life.

Once identified, you could reevaluate your wants and make sense of your current goals and aspirations. If they remain part of your goals, but you cannot move on, it is vital to get to the bottom of whatever is holding you back.

If you habitually procrastinate on everyday things like cleaning out the garage, getting an oil change, or starting the garden you have been wanting, you most likely procrastinate on more important items and goals, so you feel stuck.

Procrastination is the indicator that you're not aligned with your idea.

CHALLENGE:

Identify the areas in your life you possibly procrastinate on and reevaluate.

5 Areas	Which area has the most delay or avoidance?	Which area is costing you the most by avoiding?	What is it costing you to not follow through?
Things-home, closet, office, care, desk			
Relationships- family, friends, boss, team mates, customers, co-workers			
Health- Sleep, Diet, Exercise, meditation, Dr, Dental Visits			
Financial- spending habits, financial accounts, savings, retirement funds, will			

EXAMPLE:

Cleaning a closet begins with the intent followed by determination and executed with inspiration. "I intend to clean my closet, but first, my vibrational frequency for cleaning my closet must match that of a clean closet."

A clean closet has a positive high vibrational frequency. My current thoughts about cleaning my closet are negative, and it is on a low vibrational frequency. The vibrational difference is what is causing the negative feelings.

The solution is to talk yourself into good feelings about having a clean closet. Say things to yourself, such as "It feels good to have a clean closet," "I love to be able to find everything I need when my closet is organized." "It's easy to organize and keep my closet clean."

The next step is to do something that you do not resist doing. The following result will be wanting to clean and organize your closet.

Other goals, such as starting a new career, going back to school, taking care of your health, or changing bad habits, for example, should be treated the same way as cleaning a closet. The same principle applies.

You have the power to change your thoughts, perception, and feeling on any subject; the key is to be determined to do so, take the time to do so, and then proceed with the inspired action. You will know when you are ready because taking action feels like the next logical step.

MAKE SPACE TO CREATE

DAY-27

EVALUATING POSSIBLE DISTRACTIONS

What are some things that you may still tolerate and are distracting you from moving forward or moving faster than you are? Do you tend to start and have more than one incomplete project at a time? How about any loose ends of unfinished business, including relationships?

You have already taken responsibility for your life and found clarity about what you want. You have also done quite a bit of work up to this point, replacing old limiting beliefs and habits with new positive and self- empowering ones.

You understand that by clearing away self-made obstacles, you can move forward to focus on what is in front of you with clarity and purpose.

IT IS NOT ALWAYS ABOUT TRYING TO FIX THINGS.

Sometimes it is about starting over and creating something better. Moving what is in your way frees up time and energy to focus on your future and your ultimate goals.

Tolerating incomplete and minor irritants, as well as holding on to negative aspects of your past, will only sabotage your plans.

CHALLENGE:

- Think about things in any area of your life that you are currently tolerating.

- Think of other things in your way, a relationship, or something physical.

- Walkthrough your home, office, and car and write down the irritants and incomplete.

- Think about the solution. Is it scheduling the time for it to be dealt with? Can it be delegated to someone else or hired out?

- How about asking for help? You cannot get a yes if you do not ask.

- Having a due date on a calendar keeps you on track and focused. Have a list where you can see it often or set reminders on your smartphone.

- Check the complete box when done. Seeing the boxes checked will increase your confidence to proceed.

Example of incomplete.

- Unpaid debt
- Unorganized drawers or closet
- Messy garage
- Email clutter
- Missing or broken tools
- Electronics that need batteries
- A messy or dirty car
- Car repair or maintenance
- General clutter

- Outdated resume
- Muddy yard, overgrown weeds
- Replace batteries
- Change light bulbs
- Get a haircut
- Make doctor/ dentist appointments
- Calling your parent

Make a clearing chart like the one below to begin your process of clearing and deleting.

What is incomplete? What is irritating me?	How can I fix it?	Can all of it or part of it be delegated? If yes, to whom?	Due date	Check off

VISUALIZATION DONE RIGHT

DAY-28

VISUALIZATION IS A POWERFUL TOOL FOR SEVERAL REASONS

- It activates our subconscious mind to begin the creative process.

- It focuses the brain by programming it to notice available resources that were always there but were previously unnoticed.

- It is the first step in the attraction process, becoming a magnet to resources to help the manifestation occur.

- It helps you practice being in the NOW by visualizing in the present tense.

According to research, the mind does not differentiate between physically performing something and visualizing it. Sport Psychologists have been utilizing the power of visualization since the 1980s, and almost all Olympians and professional athletes employ visualization in their training routine.

Harvard University researchers found that students who visualized their tasks in advance of the performance had nearly 100% accuracy. Students who did not visualize had only 55% accuracy.

Children in the early stages of training, such as in gymnastics, are taught the "see it, be it" visualization technique. Before the performance, they close their eyes and envision themselves performing the task the way they wish to accomplish it.

logic will take you from A to B

IMAGINATION

will take you everywhere

INSPIRATION WILL FOLLOW VISUALIZATION

- You become aware of things that bring you closer to your goal.

- You will come up with new ideas, usually as soon as you wake up.

- You will have your best ideas while performing activities you enjoy; when you are happy and relaxed.

- You will feel motivated and energized about doing things that bring you closer to your goal.

- You get the feeling that you have to do this one thing, pick up that book, talk to that one person or go to that specific place at that particular time.

- Circumstances present themselves.

- You are at the right place at the right time.

- Things seem to fall in your lap.

- When a door closes, others open, and you begin to appreciate the blessings in disguise.

Your mind is a powerful and efficient creator that likes specifics. When you involve all your senses and feel deep emotion, you know you're doing this right.

VISUALIZATION + STRONG EMOTION + REPETITION = MANIFESTATION

VISUALIZATION IS A PROGRAMMING AND REPROGRAMMING TOOL

DR. Bruce H. Lipton, PH.D. wrote in "The Biology of Belief," "the conscious mind holds our wishes, desires, and aspirations for our lives. It is the mind that conjures up our "positive thoughts." "In contrast, the subconscious mind is primarily a repository of stimulus-response tapes derived from instincts and learned experiences. The subconscious mind is fundamentally habitual; it will play the same behavioral responses to signals repeatedly."

"The subconscious is more than a million times more powerful than the conscious mind."

Repeating something consciously or having passing memories is not enough; it must be imprinted subconsciously through emotionally felt repetitive visualization.

Are you still finding it challenging to visualize in the present tense? You most likely already do this, <u>but</u> in the negative. Do you ever have fears or insecurities about a future event? Does your mind race to the worst possible scenarios? Do you draw negative conclusions? Does your body begin to react to the negative thoughts, and your heart races, your palms sweat, you get a horrid feeling in the pit of your stomach? That is visualization done right! Visualizing optimistic present tense scenarios is just as easy.

VISION BOARD

A vision board is another valuable tool because it serves as a visual representation of what you have on your mind. The act of putting together your board solidifies your desires, makes them real, and is a constant reminder of what it is you want. It is a focus tool to keep you moving toward your goals.

BUT, remember this tool, visualizing in general, needs to be done right! When you put your board together, make sure to visualize what's on the board AS IF you have already had those things and are currently enjoying them.

CHALLENGE:

Craft Your Own Vision Board
What you will need

1. Posterboard
2. Magazines, news articles, download images
3. Scissors
4. Glue

Cut out photos, words, or statements that represent your vision. Arrange and glue them onto your poster board.

A vision board is not the only visualizing tool; a pretty box, a folder, or an album can be fun to create. Posting things up on a refrigerator or bathroom mirror can be quite effective. The constant reminder is what is essential when utilizing these tools.

Train your mind to see these things as reality by often exposing them to your board. Try it, have fun with it; you'll be many steps closer to realizing it.

FAKE IT TILL YOU MAKE IT

DAY-29

Fake it till you make it is a modern idiom that encourages you to step out of your comfort zone and pretend to be like the person you wish you were or "act" like you have the things you wish you had. The hope is to adopt a behavior that will lead you toward that future reality by pretending.

Some people may feel uncomfortable pretending that something is when it isn't... feeling like a fake, imposter, or liar. But, acting AS IF is another useful manifestation tool if done correctly.

In 1979 Ellen Langer, a Harvard Psychologist, conducted an extraordinary experiment. "Eight men in their 70s stepped out of a van in front of a converted monastery in New Hampshire. They shuffled forward, a few of them arthritically stooped, and a couple with canes. Then they passed through the door and entered a time warp. Perry Como crooned on a vintage radio. Ed Sullivan welcomed guests on a black-and-white TV. Everything inside — including the books on the shelves and the magazines lying around — were designed to conjure 1959." The New York Times Magazine

The participants not only entered a 1959 world, but they also acted and expected to be and feel as they did back then. Some of the participants walked out without canes and even looked younger.

"Faking it until you make it" does not mean lying to others. Like visualization, it's about holding present tense thoughts coupled with action and intense emotion. The mind needs this sequence to begin working on future manifestations.

Remember FEAR?, Fantasized, Experience, Appearing, Real. It is no wonder we manifest unwanted things in our life when we fantasize about unwanted

—fretting, dreading, thinking the worst of a situation until it embodies and proves us right. Fantasizing about positive things will yield the same results in the opposite direction.

When someone told me to get off my unicorn I almost fainted

CHILDHOOD GAMES

As children, we were encouraged to pretend and to use our imagination. It was a healthy process when sheets became tents and beds became boats.

Child psychologist Sally Goddard Blyth, Director of the Institute for Neuro- Physiological Psychology, wrote, "Simply put, imagination is the ability to create visual images in the mind's eye, which allows us to explore all sorts of images and ideas without being constrained by the limits of the physical world.

This is how children begin to develop problem-solving skills, coming up with new possibilities, new ways of seeing and being, which develop necessary faculties in critical thinking that will help the child throughout life".

Just because playing dress-up and pretending became unacceptable as we got older doesn't mean that the positive benefits cease to exist.

"faking it till you make it" may feel artificial at first, but once you allow yourself to imagine, the process will bring back memories of when it was encouraged to "act as if," and it eventually, it will stop feeling weird.

GOOD TIMES ARE NEVER - ENDING
WHEN WE'RE
playing and pretending

HOW TO FAKE IT TILL YOU MAKE IT

Suppose you wish to work in a bank, dress, and comport yourself as someone who works in a bank. If you are currently unemployed and know what career you want, dress the part.

Get up every morning and get dressed like you are going to work. If you sit around watching tv in your pajamas, you will likely stay watching tv in your pajamas. Make an effort to be around people in the line of work you wish to be in. Notice how they dress, how they act, and what they do. Like attracts like, and before you know it, you will no longer be faking it.

If you desire to go on a trip, do some preliminary research on the location as realistic as possible. Plan your points of interest and research local attractions. Find photos in magazines or online and look at them often.

Go further by visualizing how it feels to be on the trip. If it's a tropical beach vacation, envision the sun's warmth on your skin, the ocean's scent and sound, and how good the sand feels under your feet. Remember, the mind does not know whether you are just thinking about it or experiencing it, so it must set the manifestation in motion.

Jack Canfield, National Bestseller writer of the "Success Principles," has a mock high-end cocktail party at the end of some of his seminars.

The participants are instructed to attend in character and act as if they live their dreams and have achieved their goals. As the participants have conversations with others, they are animated, enthusiastic, and excited.

Even though the participants had yet to achieve their goal in reality, they **FELT** as if they did and displayed the corresponding emotion, all of which is needed for the manifestation to be on its way.

CHALLENGE:

- Go ahead, try it! Act as if you have achieved your goals. If you wish to be a teacher, learn about and act as a teacher; if you want to be an athlete, a world-class pianist, painter, etc., research and get into character.

- If you want to drive a certain vehicle, go to the dealership and test drive one, all while imagining you already own it.

- Successful people have self-confidence, don't worry about what others think; besides, you will do the exercise whenever you choose.

What you think you create, What you feel you attract, What you imagine you become

FACE YOUR FEARS

DAY-30

Fear can be debilitating and will stop you in your tracks, and although you understand that Fear is Fantasized Experiences Appearing Real, it still takes work to get over specific fears, so how will you do this?

- First, you face it. Make a note of what you continue to be fearful of.
- Second, make a concrete plan to overcome that fear.

CHALLENGE:

Make a list of the things you are afraid to do. (not of things you are scared of).

For example, I am afraid to;

Everything you're running away from is in your head

- Ask for a raise
- Ask someone out for a date
- Ride a rollercoaster
- Have children
- Leave this job that I hate
- Start my own business

Using the format below, restate each fear.

I want to_____, but I scare myself by imagining_____.

EXAMPLE:

"I want to learn how to ski, but I scare myself by imagining that I won't be able to stop and break my leg."

Note that you are self-creating your fear by imagining a negative outcome. Next: Write down the statements one more time; imagine a positive outcome this time.

Example: "I want to learn how to ski, and I imagine myself successfully mastering the skill, going down the hill with confidence and grace."

Don't just write; dig in and imagine the positive outcome. Use the visualization technique you've learned.

Old habits have a way of creeping in if we let them. Constant maintenance and positive focus are required if you are to succeed.

LEARN TO ASK

DAY-31

DON'T LET FEAR KEEP YOU FROM ASKING

Asking the universe for what you want may be simpler than asking another person for help. Asking others for assistance and support is a challenge because it's a risk.

Do you stop yourself from taking action and asking for something from someone due to fear of hearing the word no and feeling embarrassed, rejected, and humiliated, not wanting to seem needy, foolish, or stupid?

It's not necessary nor wise to do everything on your own. We all need one another at some point. You've likely been there for others who have come to you for help or assistance in one form or another. As you were compelled to help them, many will be happy to help you.

Do not let fear or pride get in the way of fulfilling your dreams and achieving your goals. Be genuine, put yourself out there, trust the laws of the universe to have your back. Know that your inner being is guiding you every step of the way, even to those that can help.

Successful people make it a habit to ask for what they want confidently and aren't afraid of rejection. Stop getting in your way and ask!

THE ART OF ASKING

Don't assume that the answer will be no. Remember, the law of attraction makes sure you get what you think about, and so if you think you are going to get a no, a no, you will get it.

Instead of assuming the worst, take the risk. Remember that whatever the outcome, it was for the best; besides, nothing is lost if the answer is no. If the answer is yes, you have gained. Either way, you will not know until you ask.

Asking may be the difference between an upgrade on a plane, a hotel, or theater seats. Maybe a raise, an assignment, time off, discounts, a date, or marriage.

Taking personal responsibility for your life includes being responsible for, opening your mouth and asking when appropriate. Jack Canfield and Mark Victor Hansen have written a book entitled "The Aladdin Factor," all about the science of asking for what you want and need in life. Here are a few tips from that book.

1. Ask as if you expect to get it. Ask with a positive expectation. Ask from the place that you have already been given it. It's a done deal. Ask as if you expect to get a yes.

2. Assume you can. Please don't start with the assumption that you can't get it. If you are going to assume anything, assume you can get an upgrade. Imagine you can get a table by the window. Assume that you can return it without a sales slip. Assume that you can get a scholarship, get a raise and get tickets at this late date. Don't ever assume against yourself.

3. Ask someone who can give it to you, qualify the person. "Who would I have to speak to?" "Who is authorized to decide about....." "What would have to happen for me to get....."

4. Be clear and specific.

5. Ask repeatedly. One of the most important principles of success is persistence, not giving up. Whenever you're asking others to participate in fulfilling your goals, some people are going to say no. They may have other priorities, commitments, and reasons not to participate. It's not a reflection on you. Just get used to the idea that there's going to be some rejection along the way. The key is not to give up. When someone says no, you keep on asking. Why?

Because when you keep on asking—even the same person again and again —you might get a yes....

- On a different day

- When you have new data to present

- After you've proven your commitment to them

- When circumstances have changed

- When the person trusts you more

Herbert True, a marketing specialist at Notre Dame University, found that:

- 44% of all salespeople quit trying after the first call

- 24% quit after the second call

- 14% quit after the third call

- 12% quit trying to sell their prospect after the fourth call

This means that 94% of all salespeople quit after the fourth call. But 60% of all sales are made after the fourth call. This revealing statistic shows that 94% of all salespeople don't give themselves a chance at 60% of the prospective buyers.

IF YOU DON'T ASK

the answer will always be no

FINAL CHALLENGE:

What do you need to ask for to accomplish your goals? Next to each item, make a list; write down how you stop yourself from asking, what it costs you not to ask, and what benefit you would get if you were to ask.

EXAMPLE:

A Raise: I'm afraid my boss will know I need the money. My pride is getting in my way and costing me the raise I deserve. The raise will help pay more bills and release stress at home.

A loan: I'm afraid to apply for a loan because I don't think I have a good enough credit score. Renting is more expensive than buying. I'm wasting money. Owning my own home is satisfying because It is an investment in our future.

PERSEVERANCE

Per·se·ver·ance
/ˌpərsəˈvirəns/
noun

1. persistence in doing something despite difficulty or delay in achieving success.

YOU DID IT! You completed the challenge, and you should be proud of yourself. It is not always easy to follow the methods you learned, especially in the midst of daily issues and circumstances beyond your control. There will always be something or someone on your path that will provide you with contrast, and that's a good thing.

You know how to turn a negative into a positive as a powerful creator. You know how to guide your thoughts and listen to your inner being. You have learned how to pivot and focus. You have taken responsibility, and you finished what you started. You have persevered.

Change is a process, and unfortunately, some people eventually go back to their old habits despite completing the challenge. It is sometimes difficult to overcome as stubborn and impatient humans, but don't give up if you stumble! Pull yourself together and start again; It is never too late!

Take the necessary steps to maintain your momentum, not some of the time, all of the time, especially on the good days. Regardless of internal turmoil, external circumstances, or setbacks, you can make this new mindset a life habit.

- Redo the challenge: Reinforce what you've learned. The longer you practice your new way of thinking and habits, the greater your chances of long-term success.

- Read back through individual lessons: Index the challenges and review them from time to time; you will be encouraged by your progress.

- Continue to write in your appreciation journal. Make this a self-care ritual. It will serve as a daily reminder that life is good and full of possibilities.

- Share what you have learned with others: sharing is another powerful reinforcement tool. It will help keep you accountable, and it will go a long way in ensuring a stable footing and a successful future.

You have the power to make things happen! Continue practicing the actions that have gotten you this far.

Happy

is a choice
and success is optional

Terrific work! You are a powerful creator with many desires, hopes, and dreams, and no one can keep you from progressing and living a happy, abundant, and fulfilling life.

I hope this workbook met your expectations and that the challenges have helped expand your mind to a world of endless possibilities.

I'm confident that if you continue to apply the principles you've learned, you will not only live but thrive!

Many hugs and well wishes,

Claudia

LAW OF ATTRACTION CAMP

SUGGESTED READING LIST

Abraham Hicks
- The law of Attraction
- Ask, and it is Given
- The Astonishing Power of Emotions
- The Amazing Power of Deliberate Intent
- The Vortex

John Kehoe
- Mind Power into the 21st Century: Techniques to Harness the Astounding
- Powers of Thought
- The Practice of Happiness
- Quantum Warrior: The Future of the Mind

Dr. Bruce Lipton
- The Biology of Belief
- The Honeymoon Effect: The Science of Creating Heaven on Earth

Jack Canfield
- Success Principles
- The Alladin Factor: How to Ask for What You Want and Get It

Nick Ortner
- The Tapping Solution: A Revolutionary System for Stress-Free Living

DOCUMENTARIES

- Heal, a Netflix Original
- The Secret (the original version)

Printed in the United States
by Baker & Taylor Publisher Services